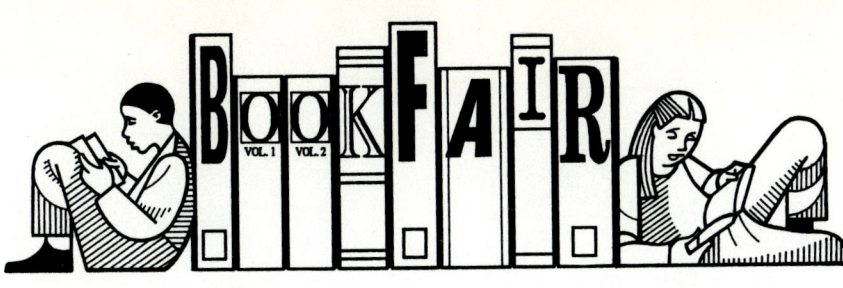

MW01599030

TODAY'S ASSIGNMENT IS...

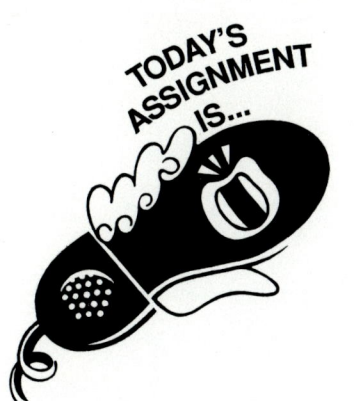

TODAY'S ASSIGNMENT IS...

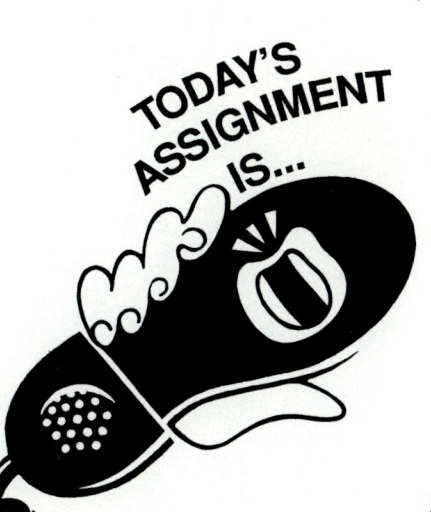

TODAY'S ASSIGNMENT IS...

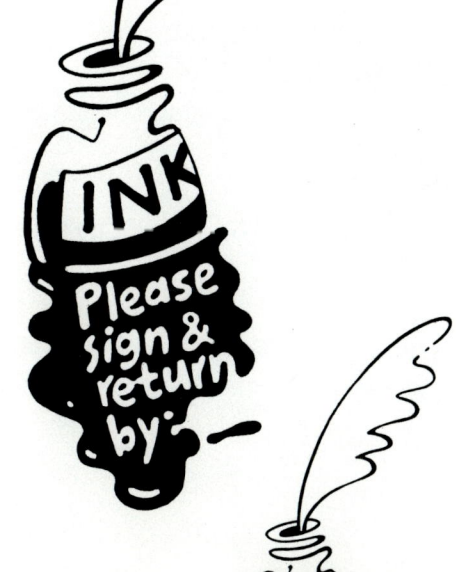

INK

Please sign & return by:

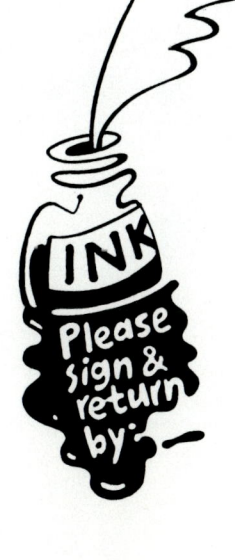

INK

Please sign & return by:

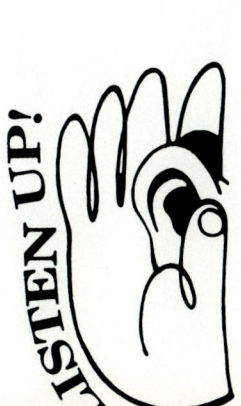

INK

Please sign & return by:

LISTEN UP!

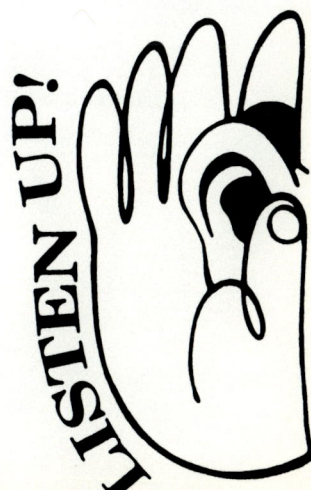

LISTEN UP!

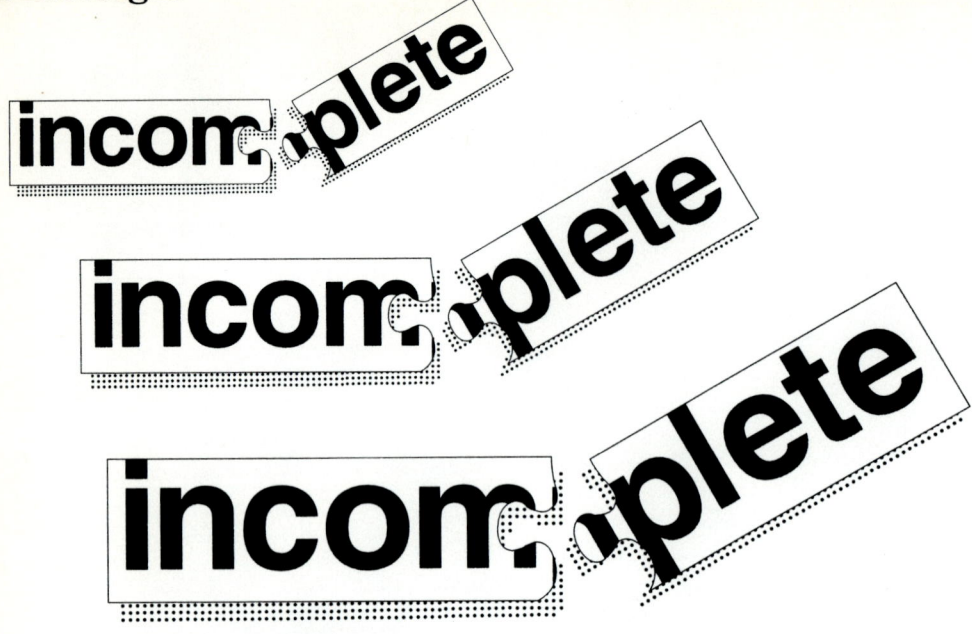

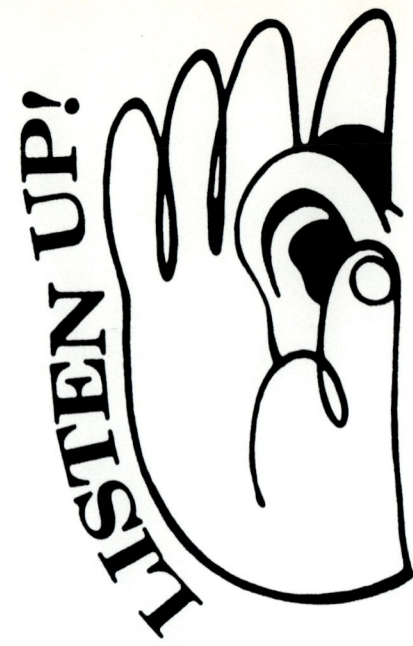

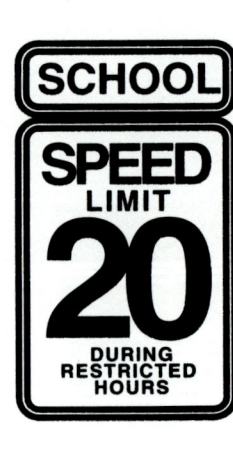

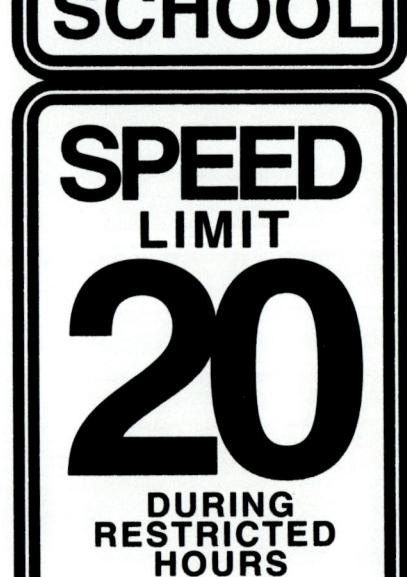

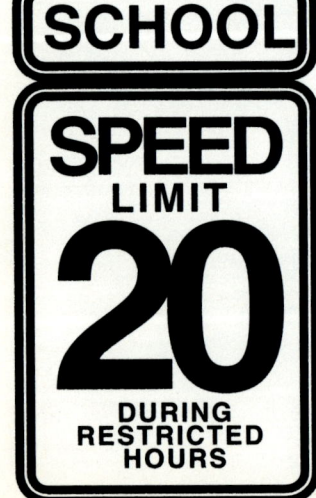

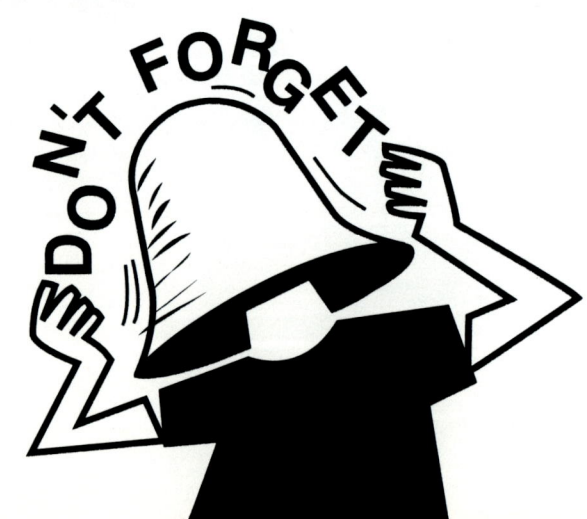

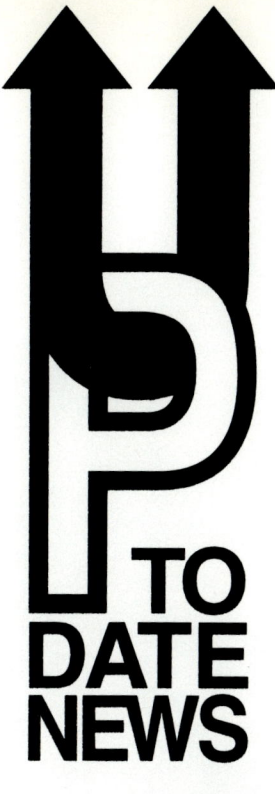

UP TO DATE NEWS

READ THIS

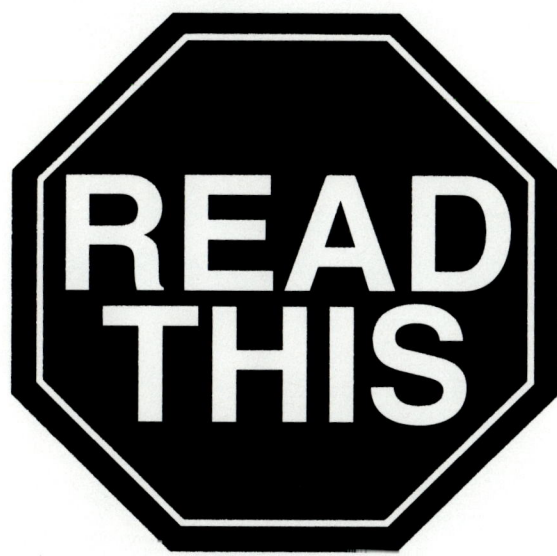

READ THIS

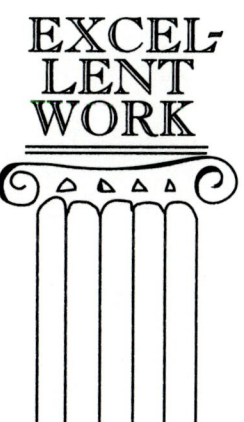

UP TO DATE NEWS

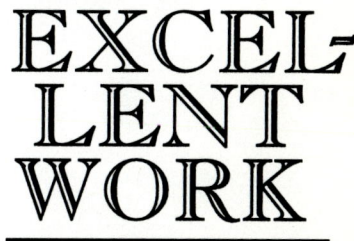

EXCELLENT WORK

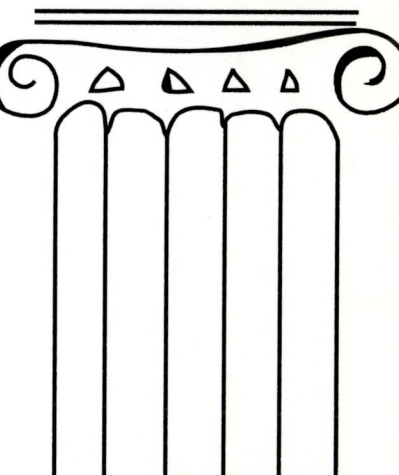

EXCELLENT WORK

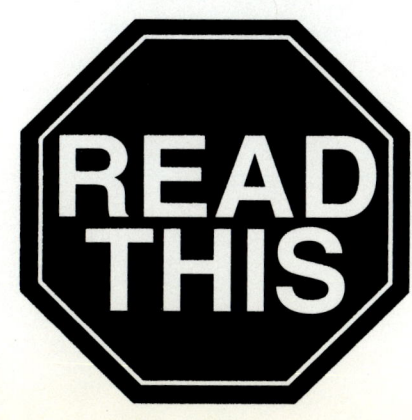

READ THIS

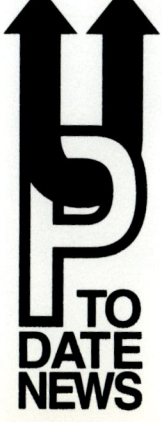

UP TO DATE NEWS

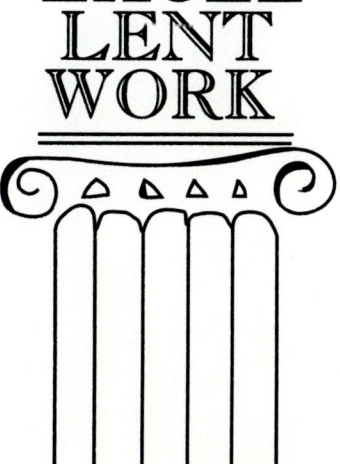

EXCELLENT WORK

READ THIS

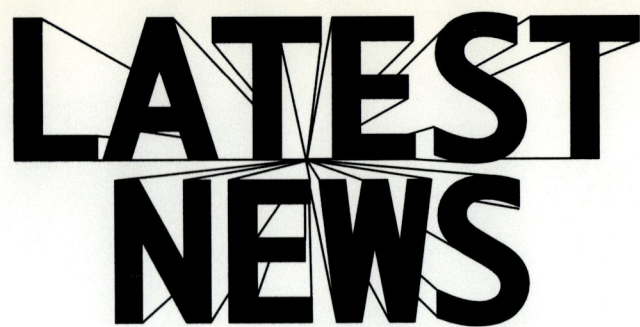

SCIENCE FAIR

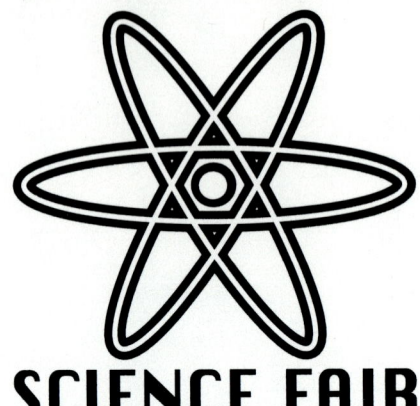

SCIENCE FAIR

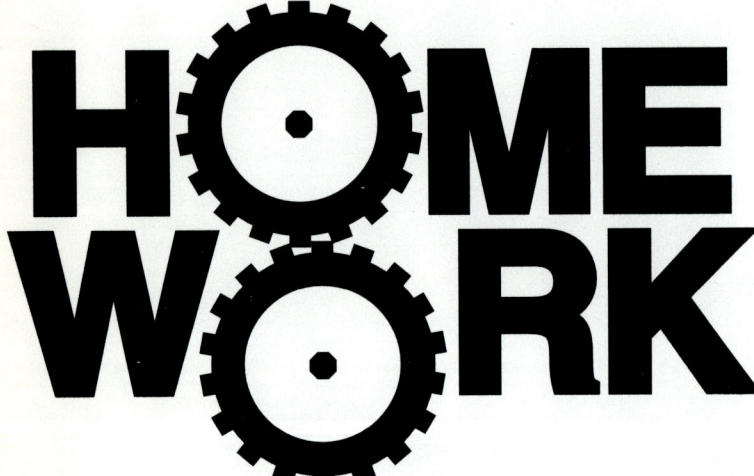

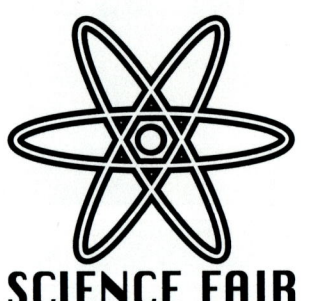

SCIENCE FAIR

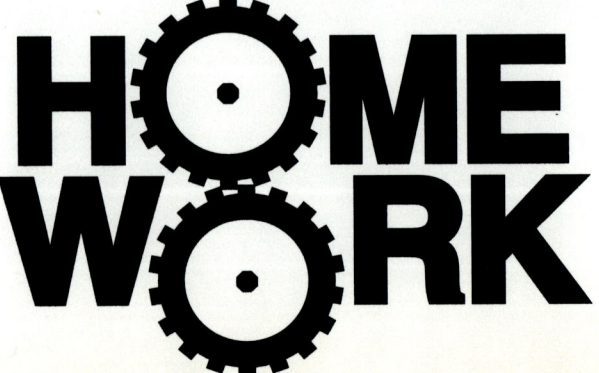

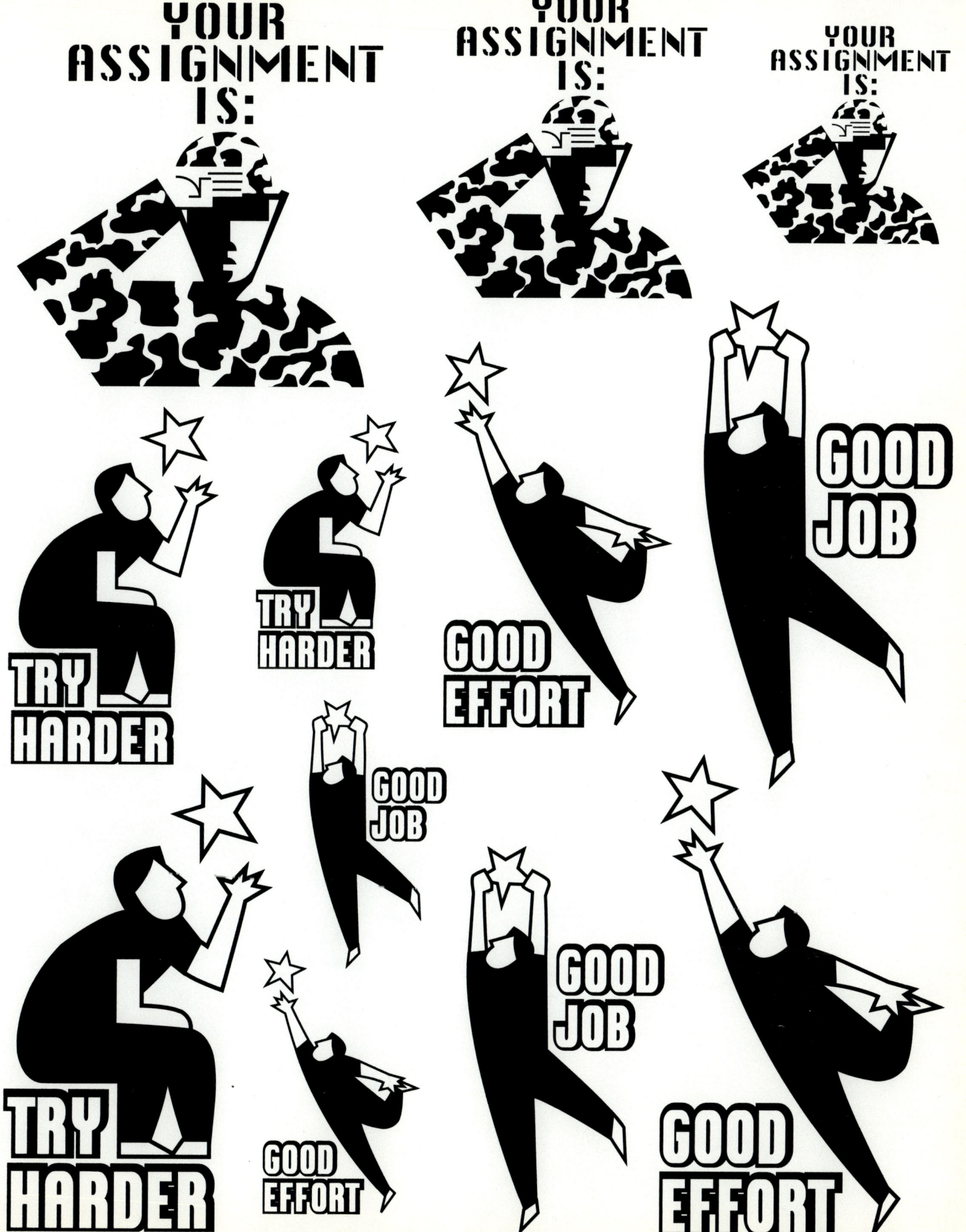

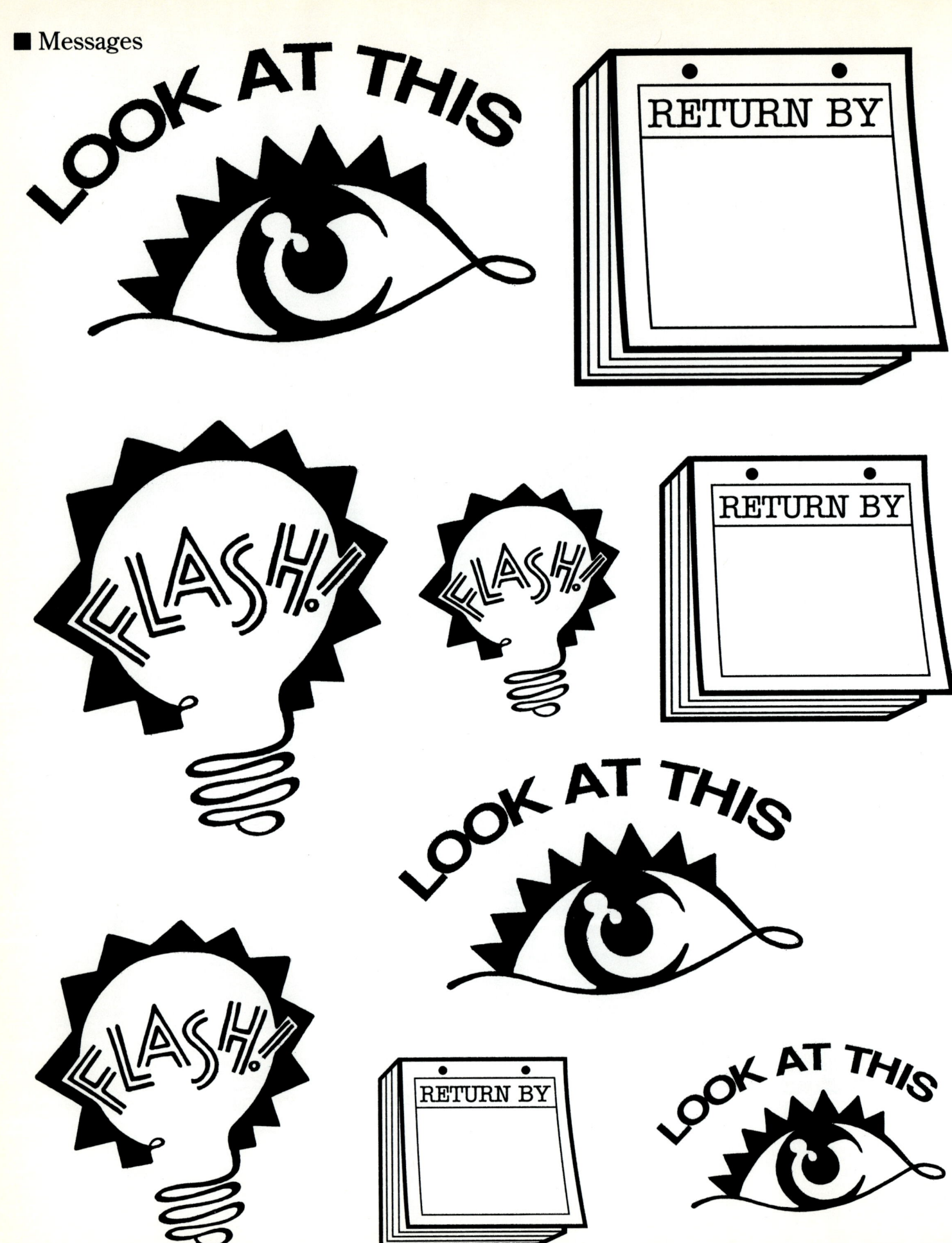

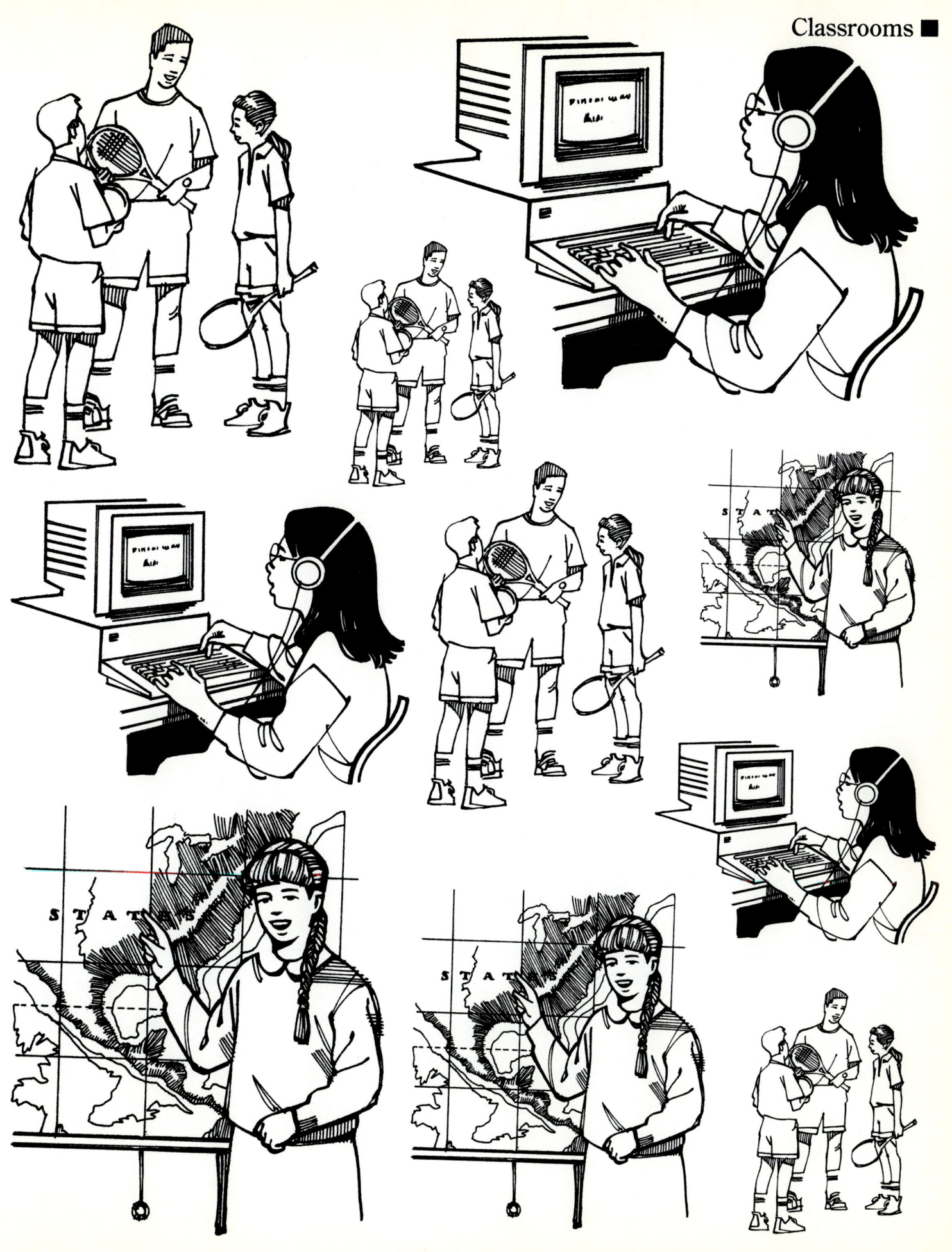

■ Classrooms

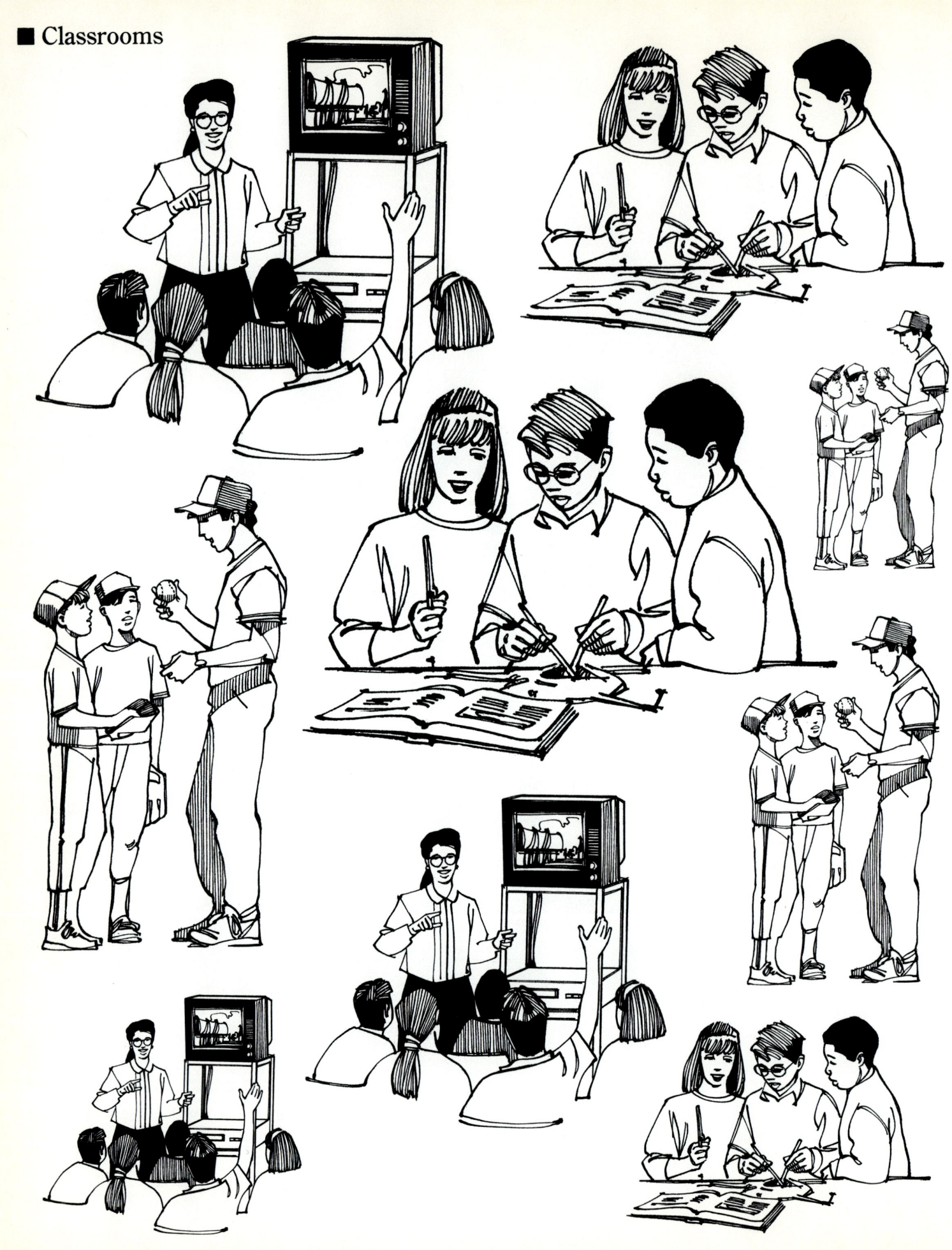

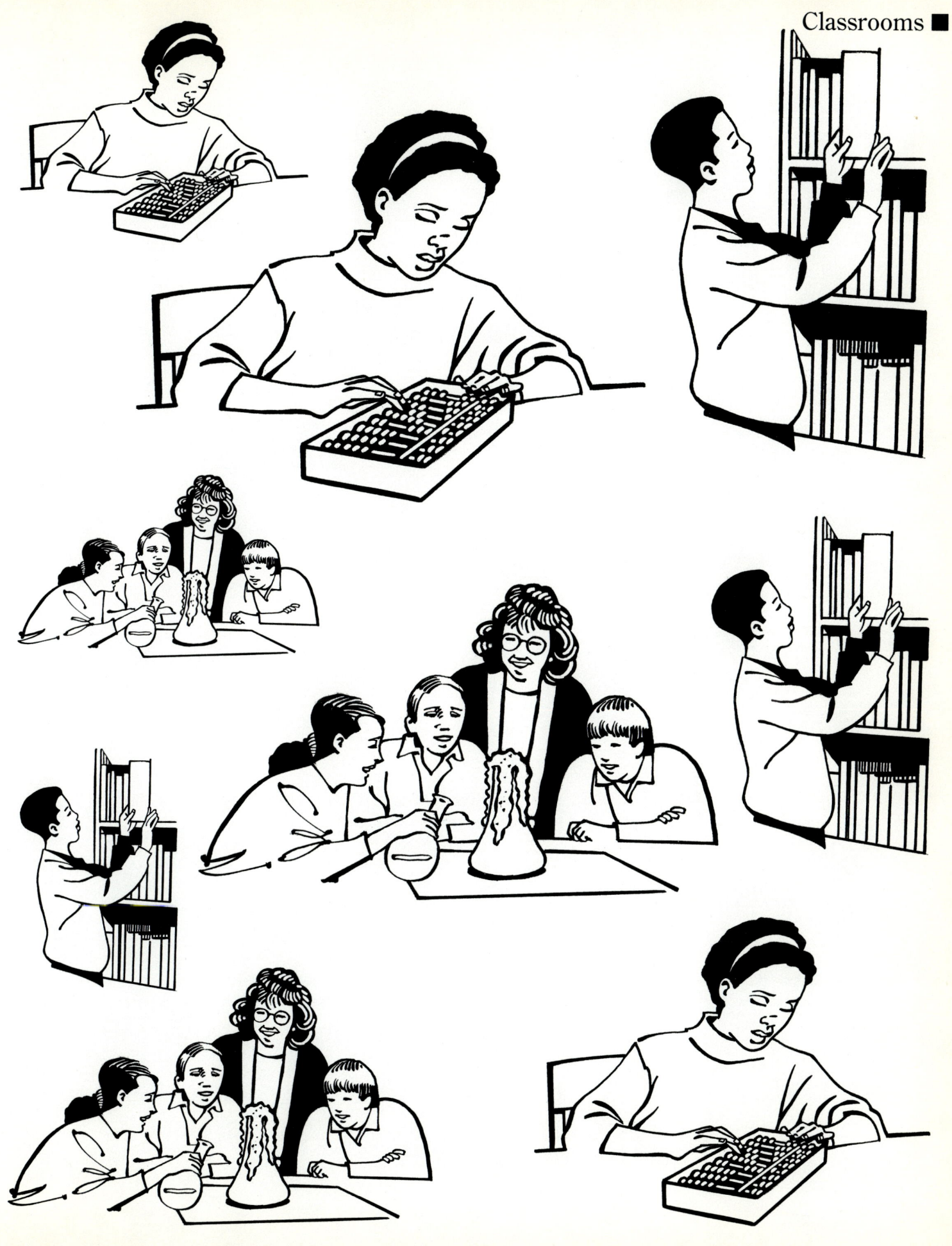

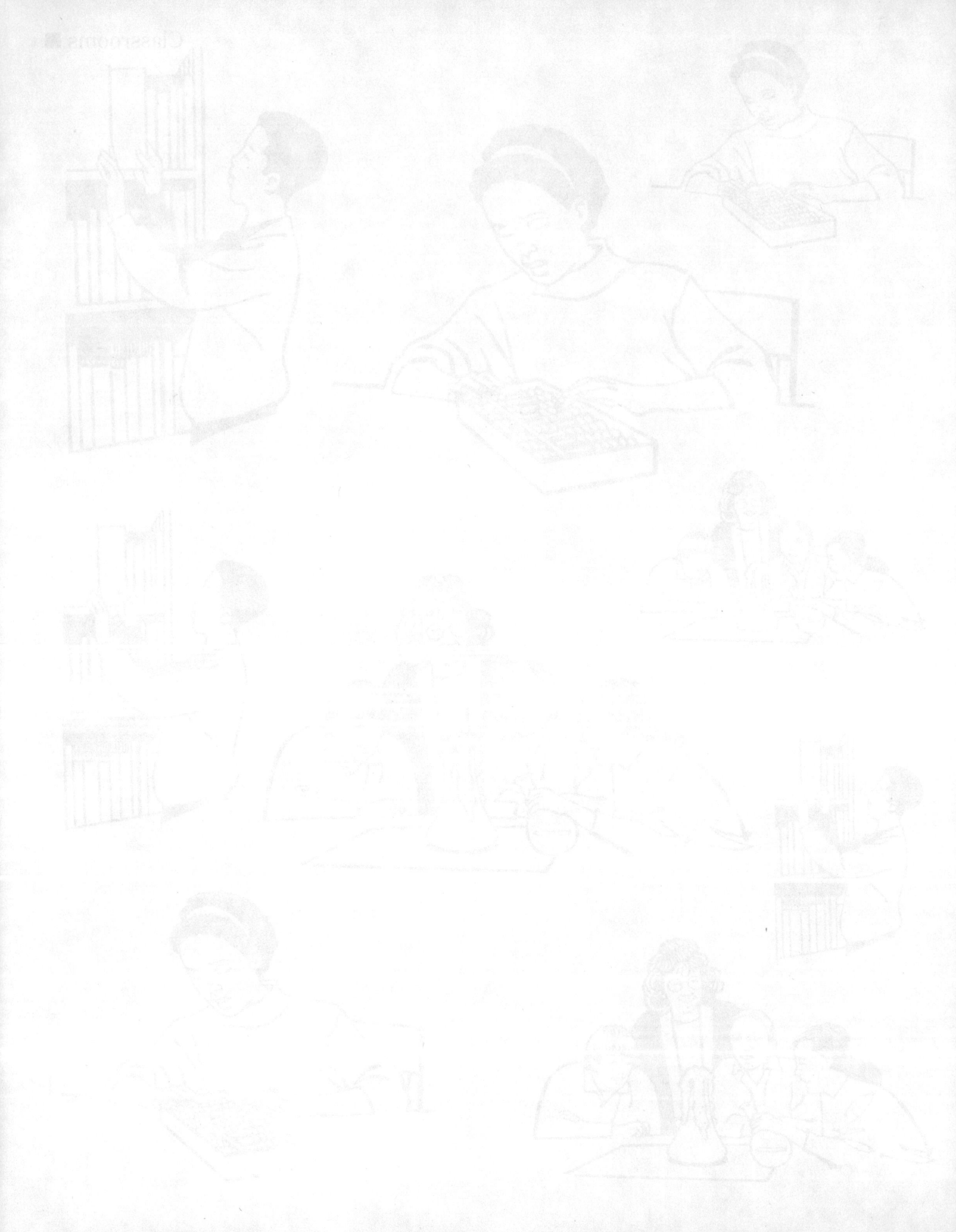

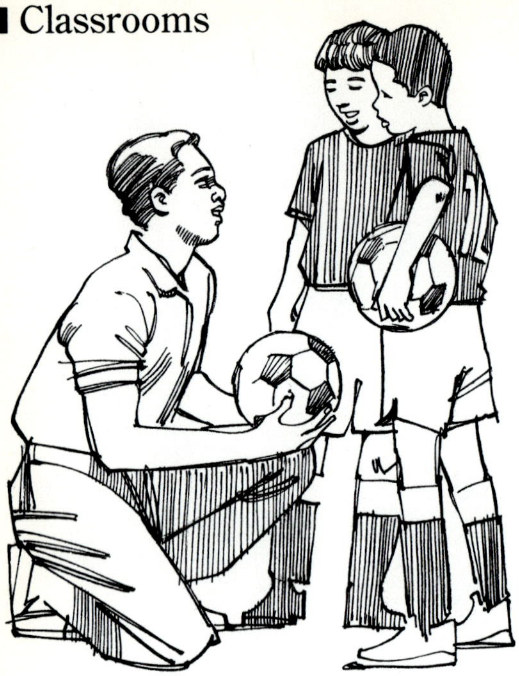

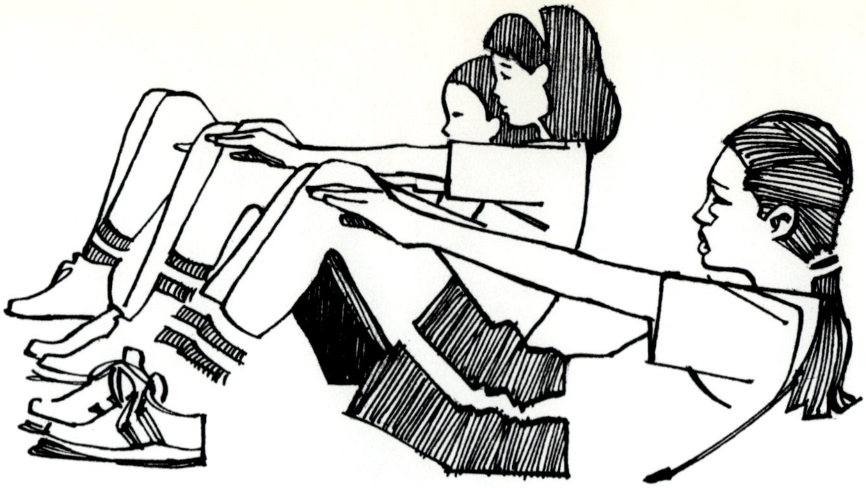

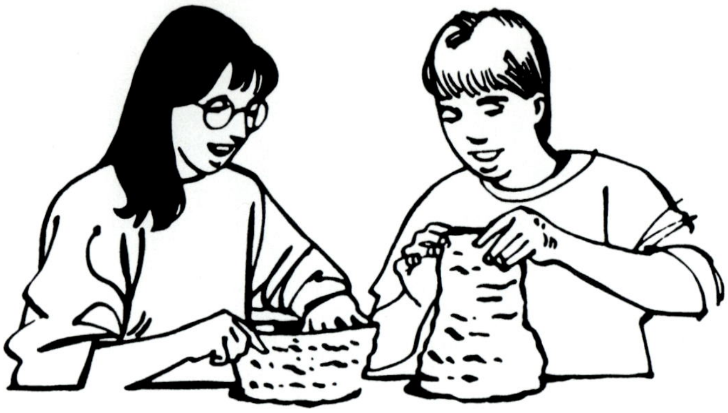

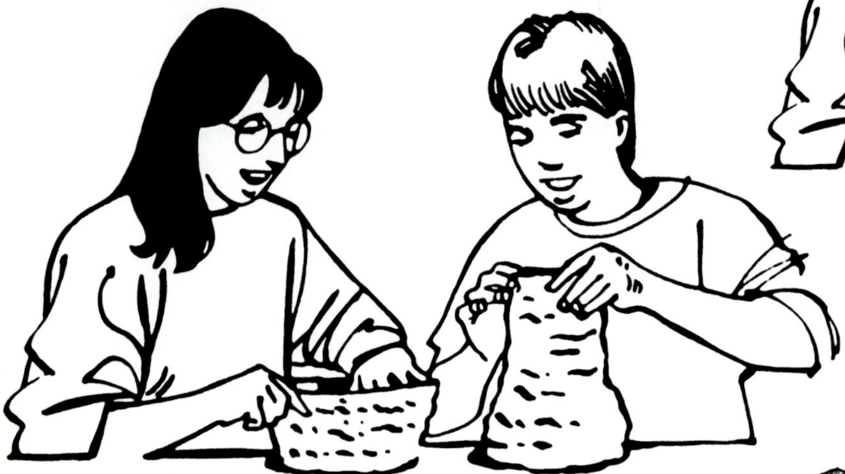

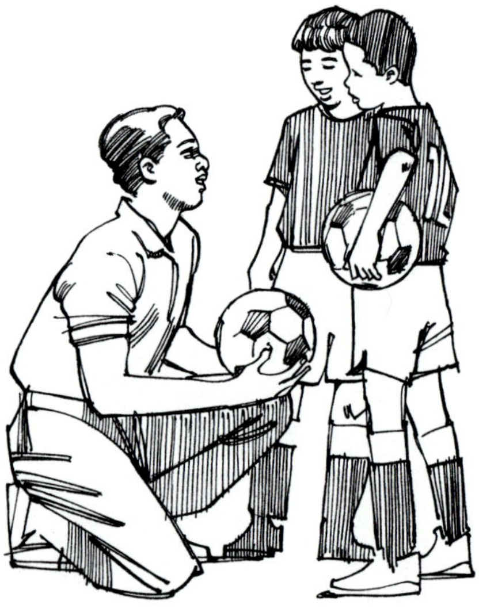

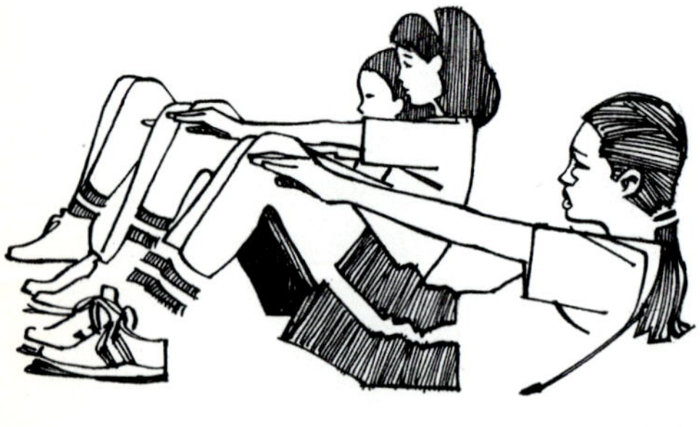

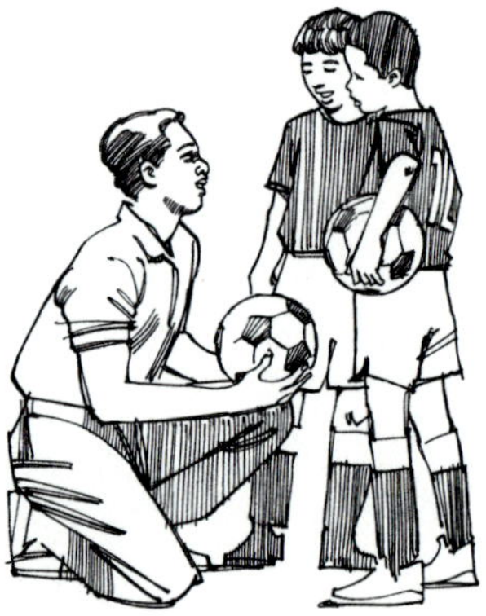

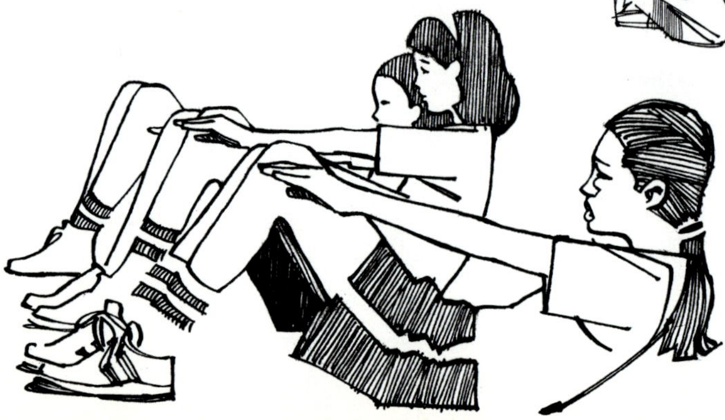

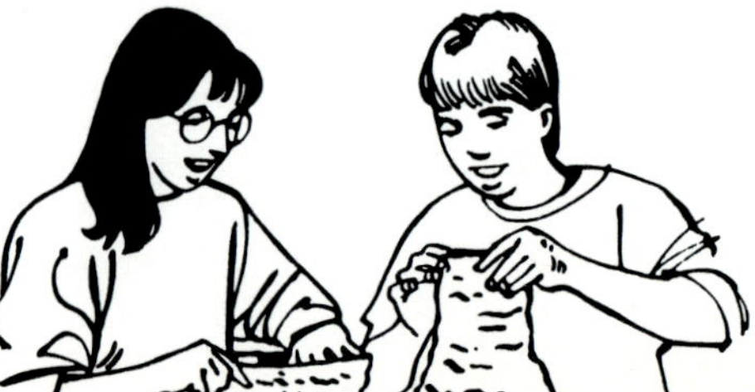

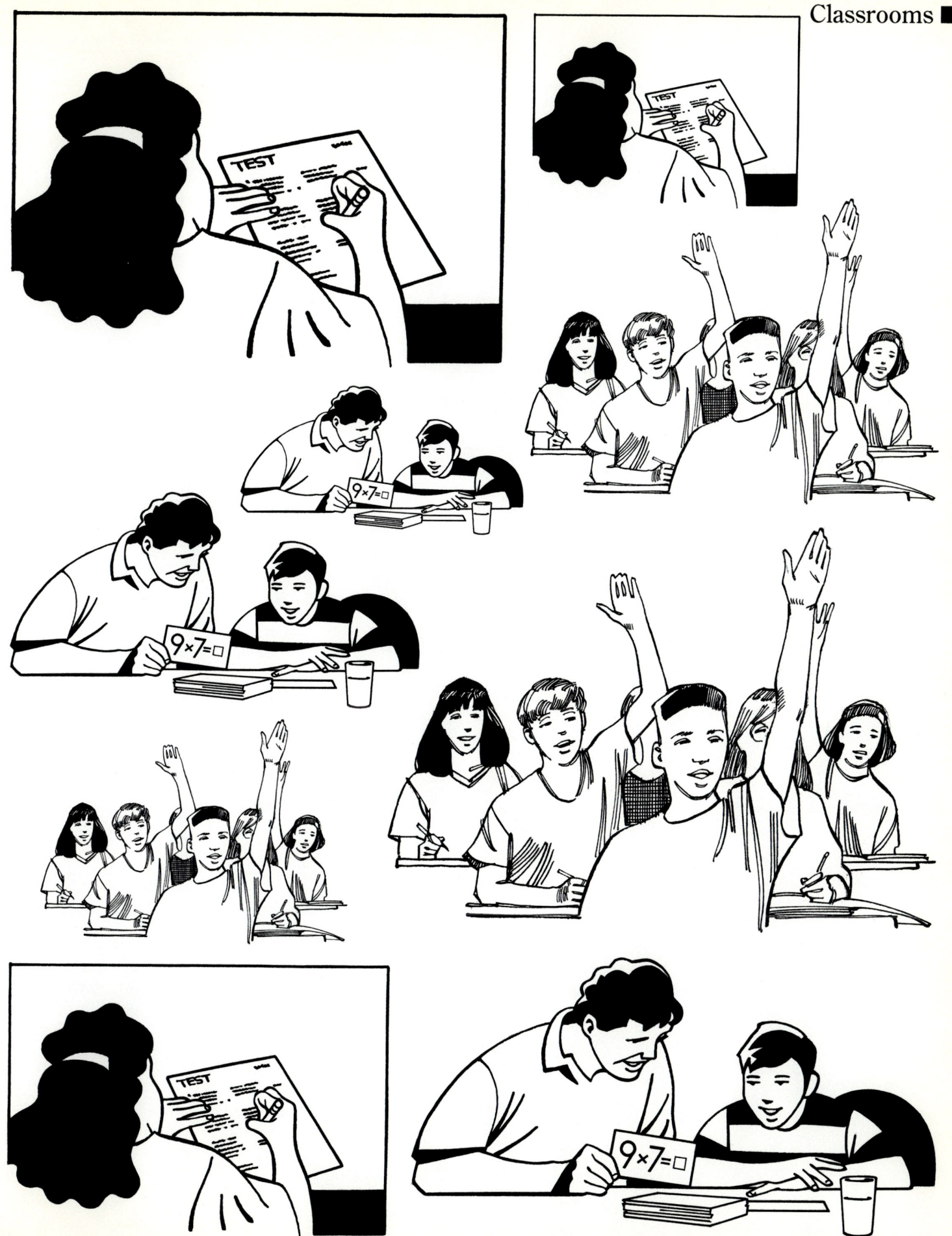

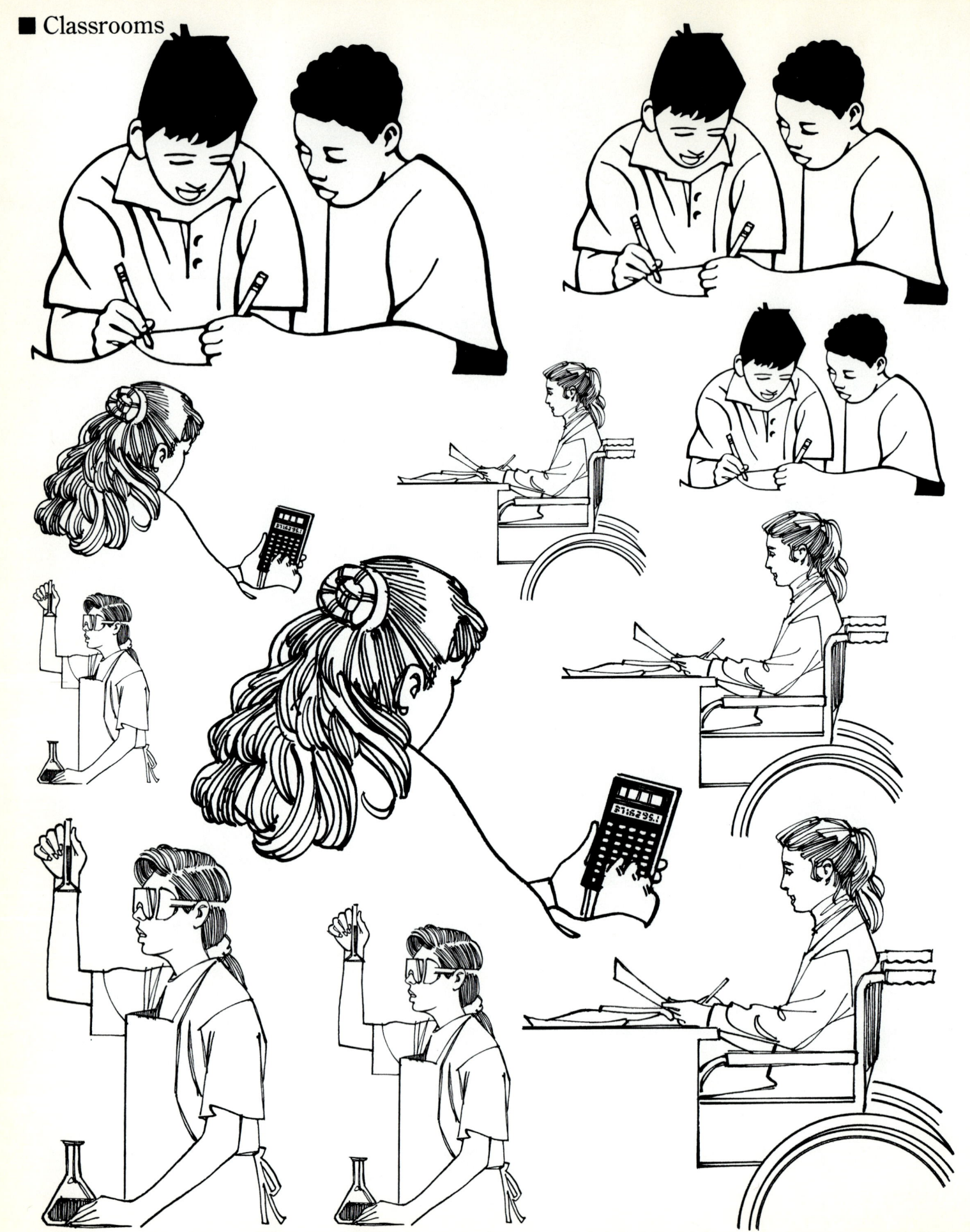

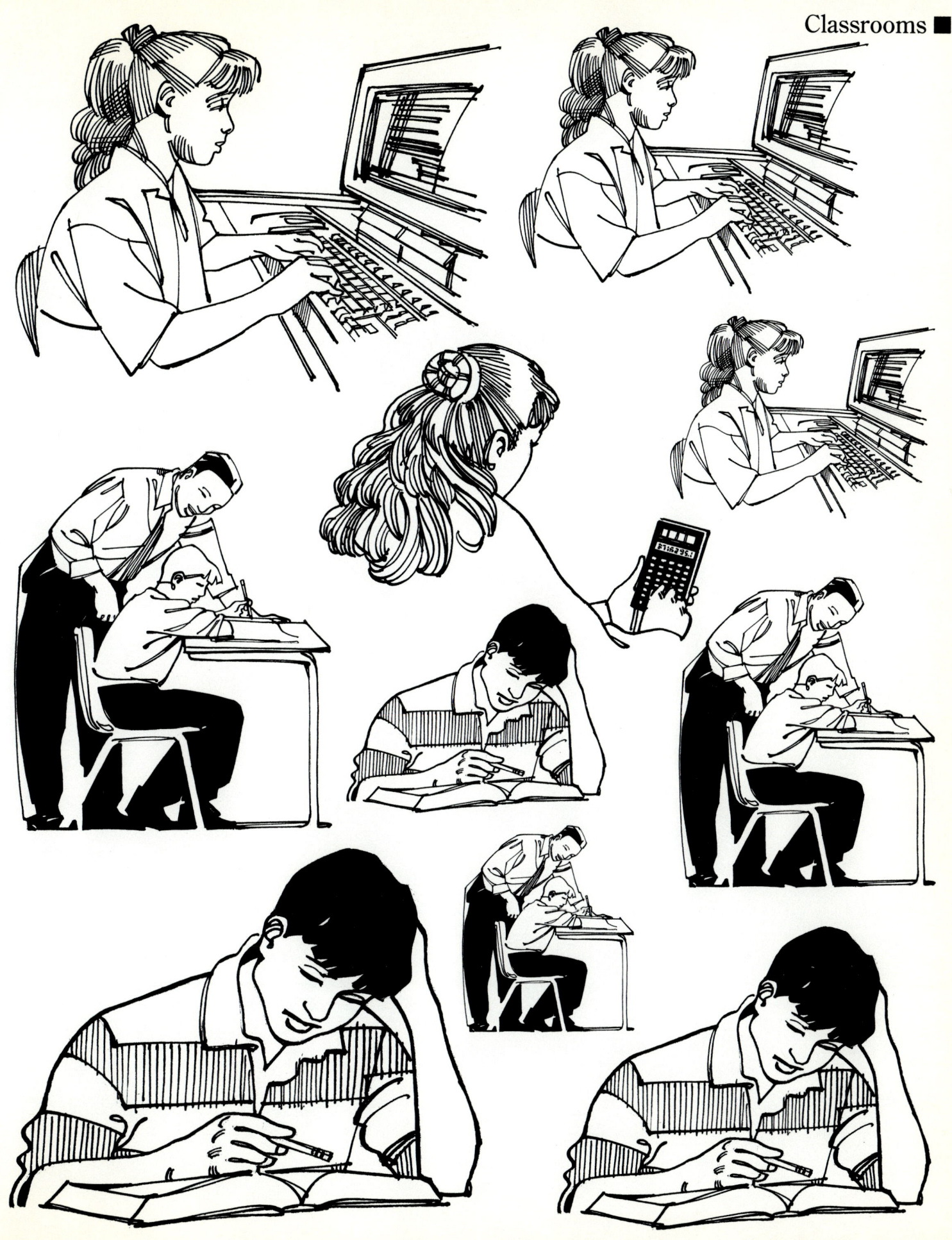

■ Classrooms

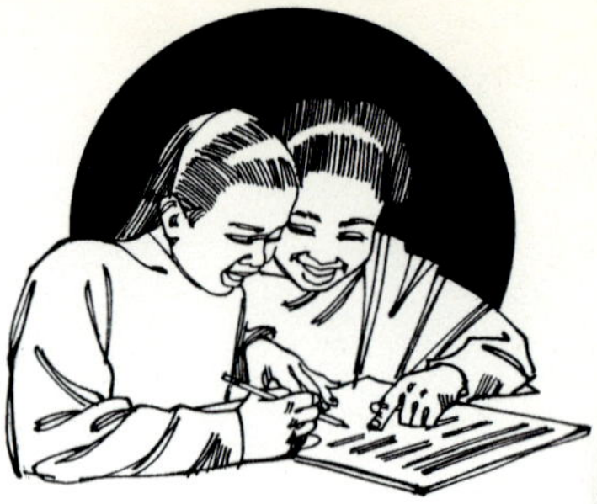

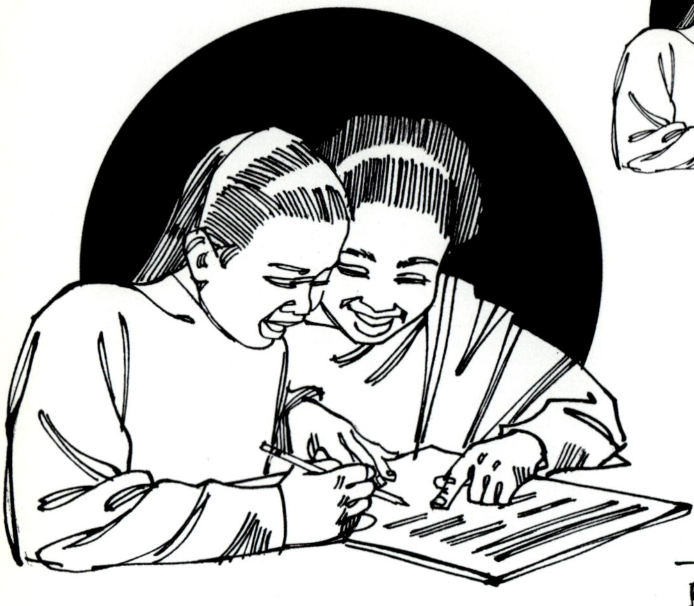

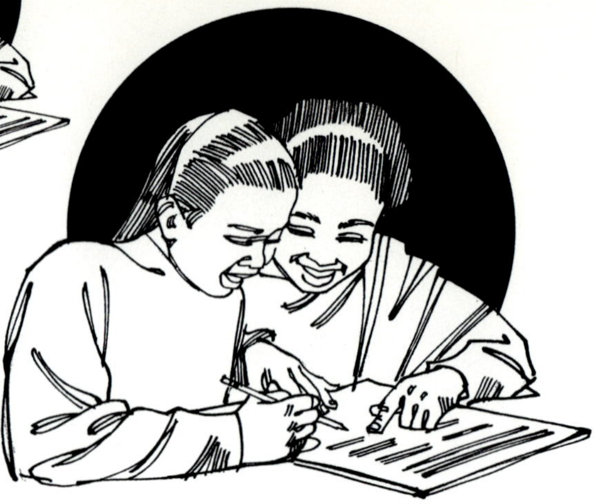

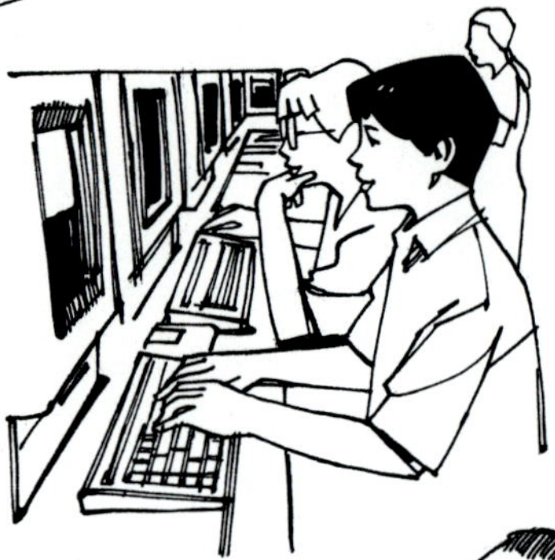

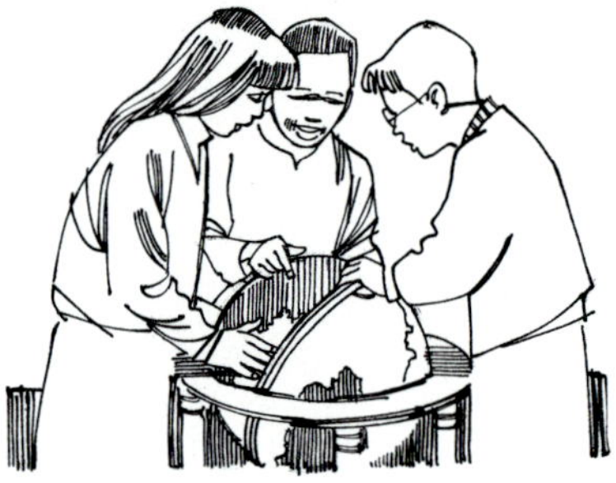

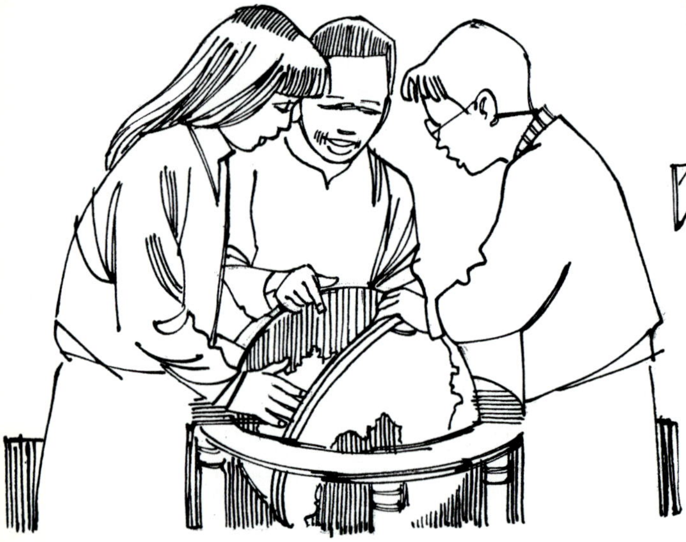

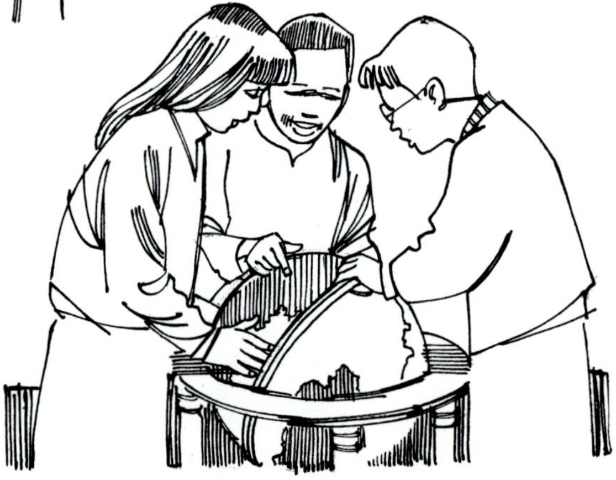

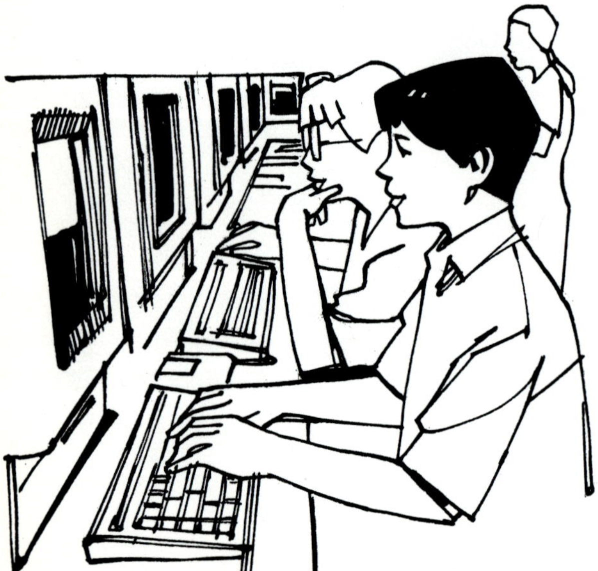

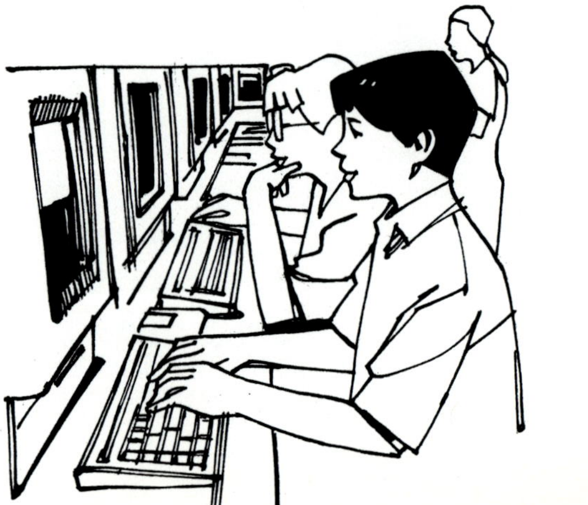

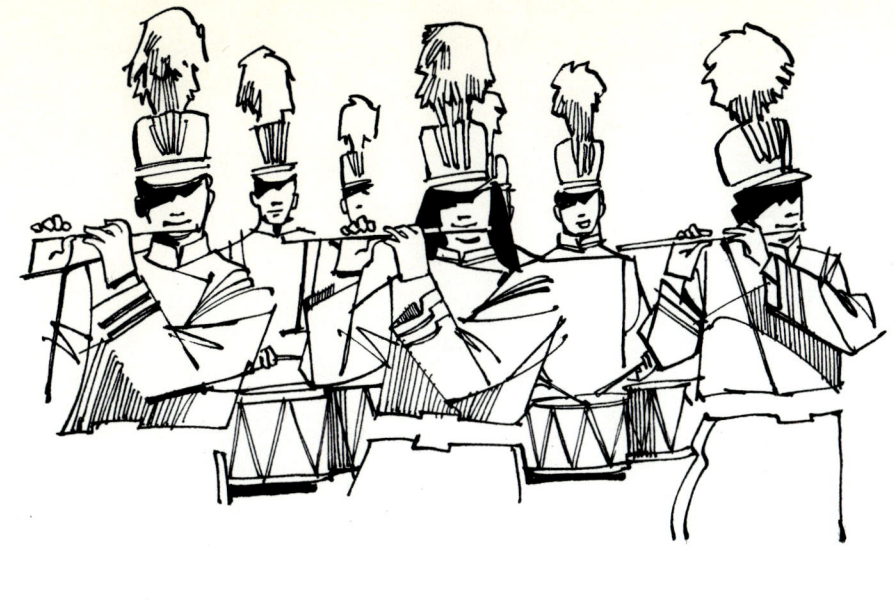

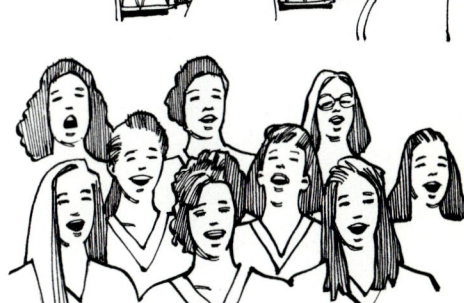

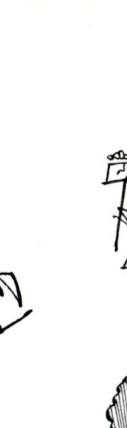

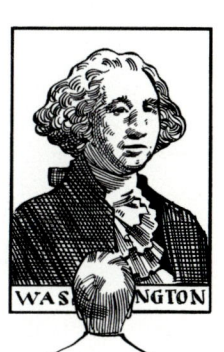

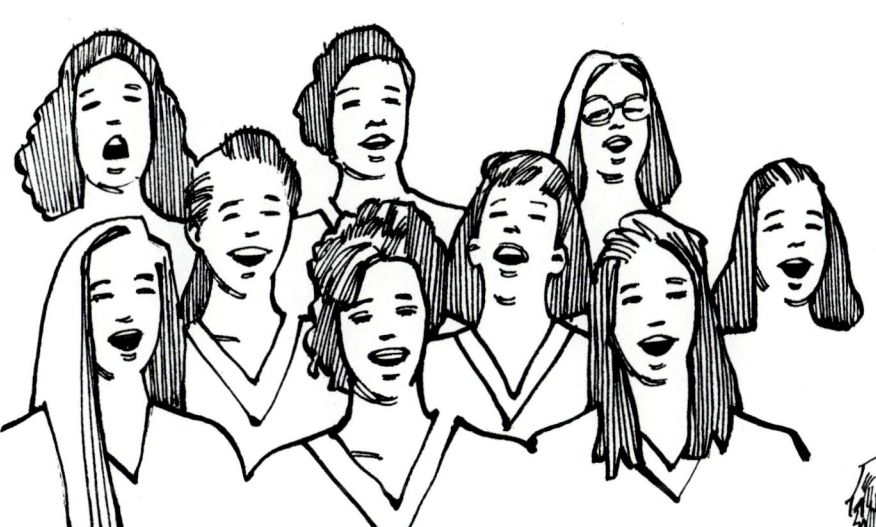

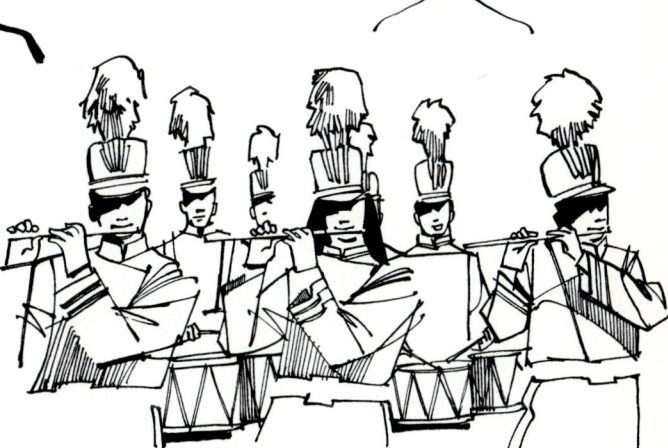

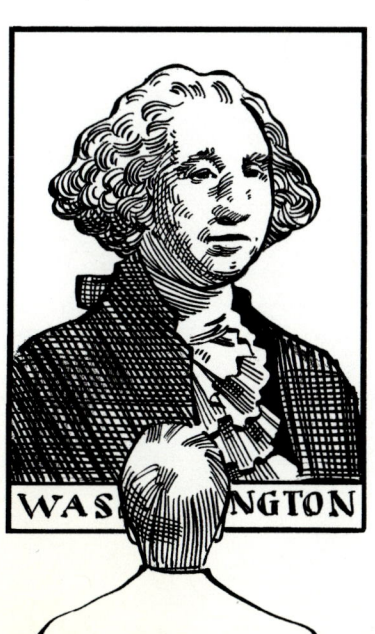

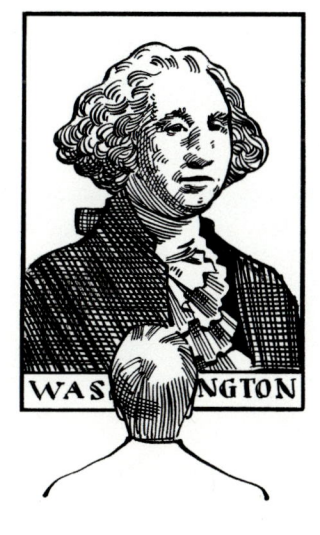

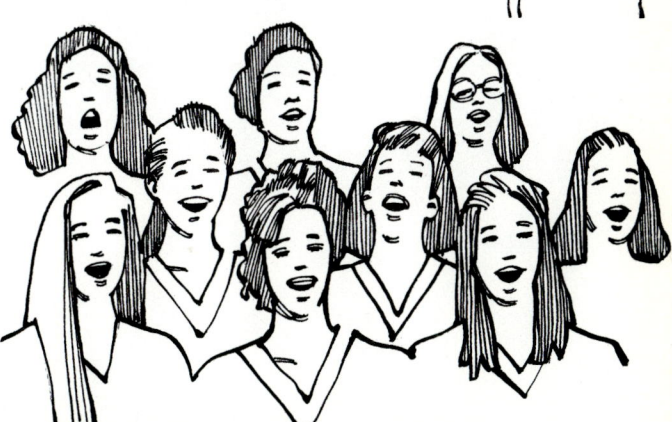

School Situations

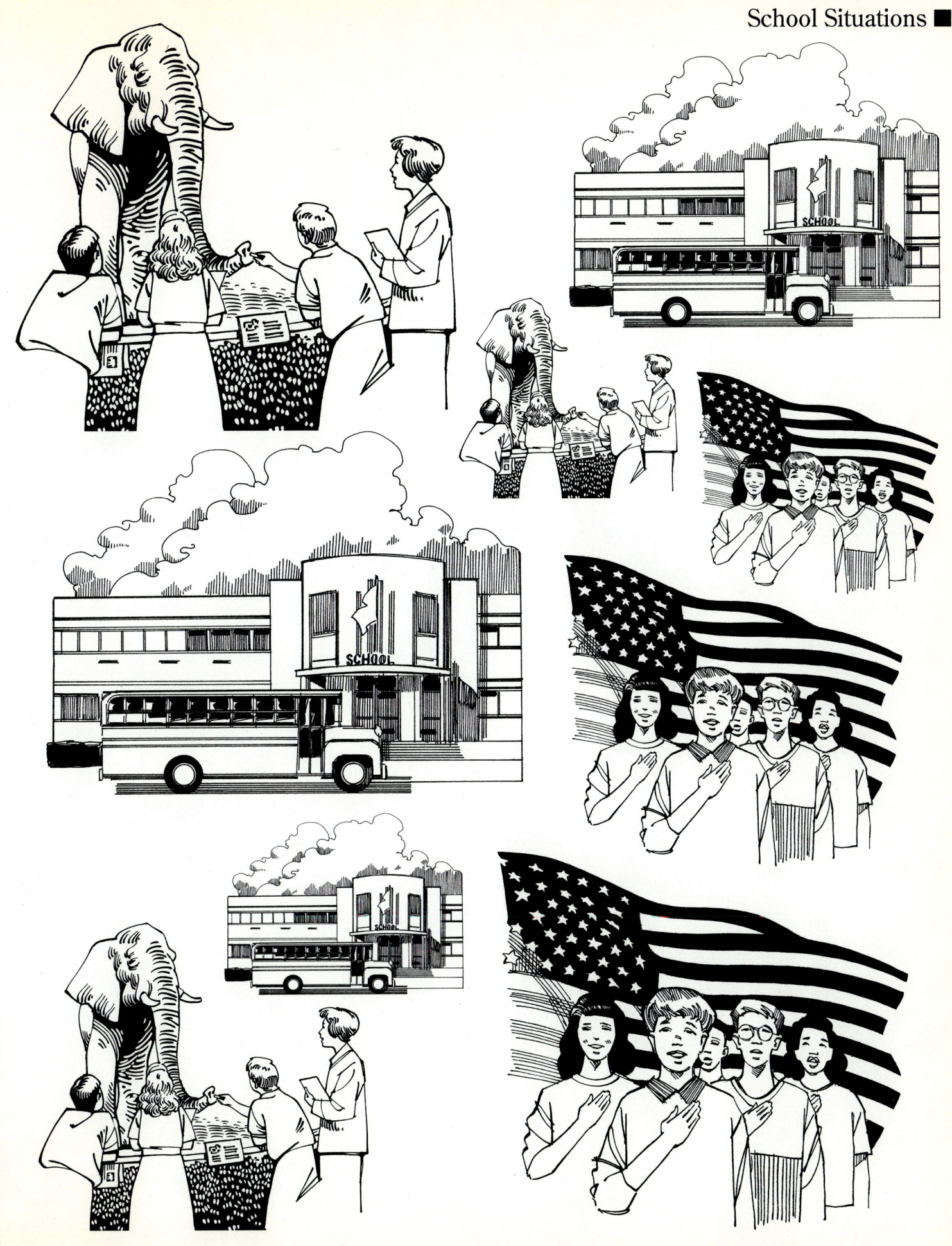

■ School Situations

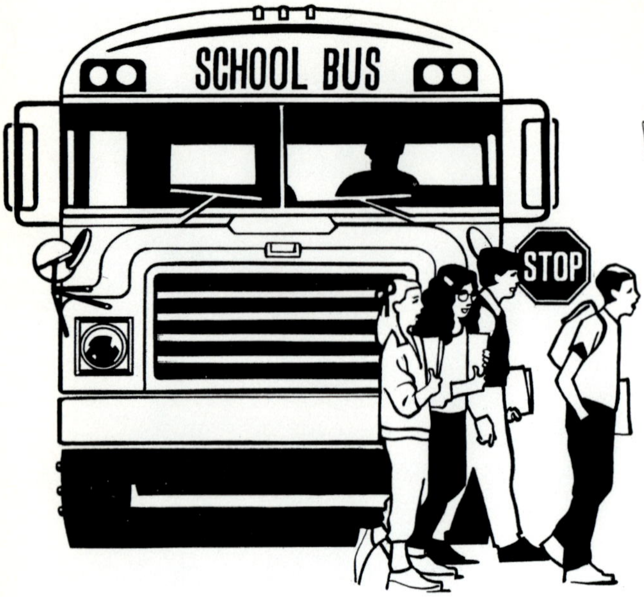

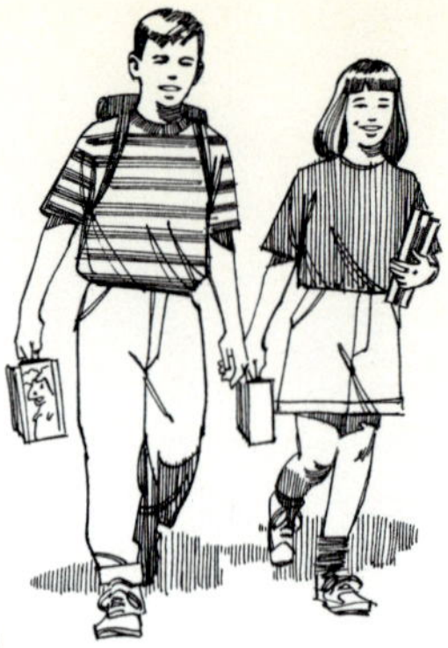

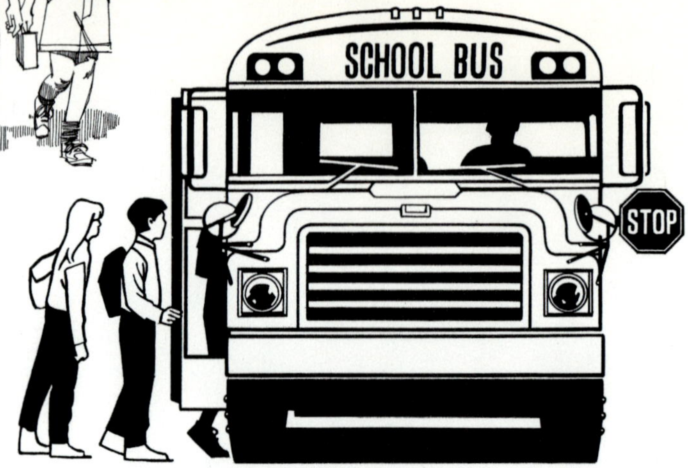

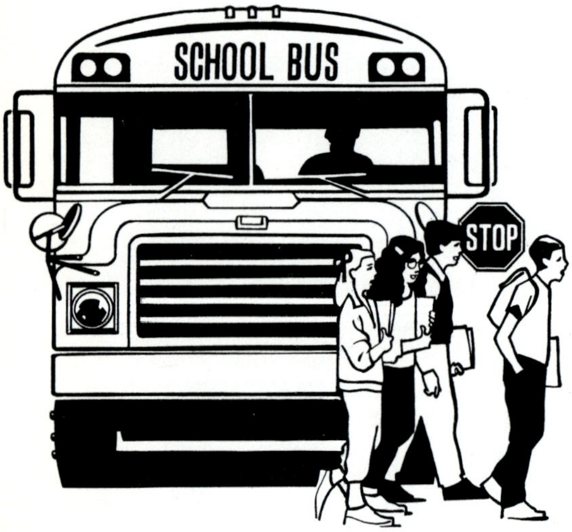

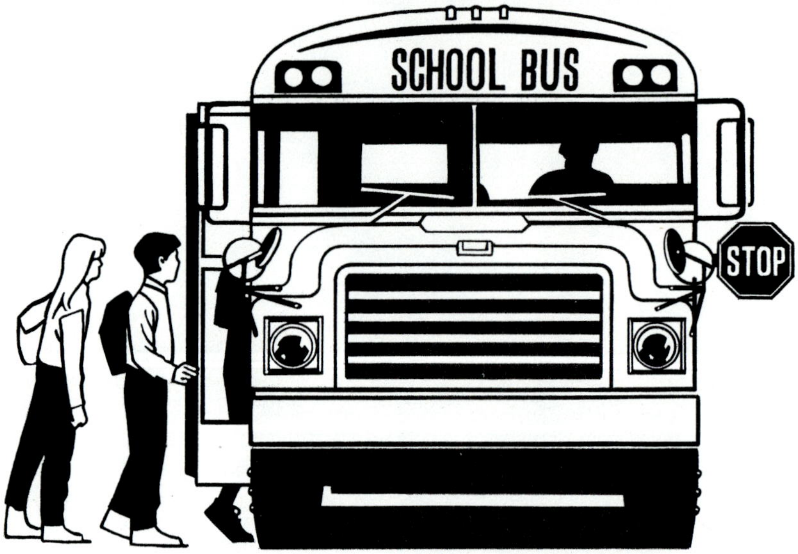

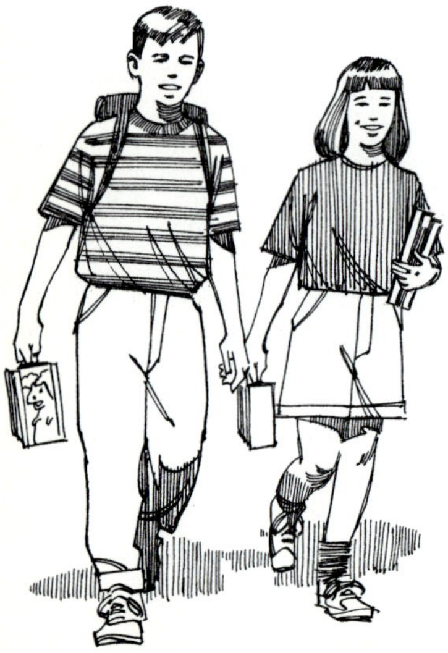

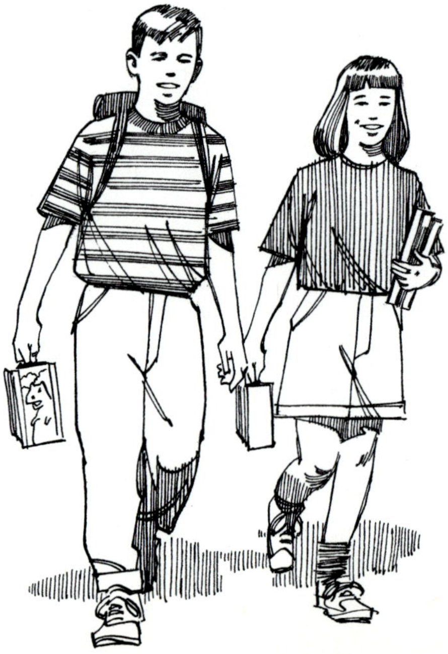

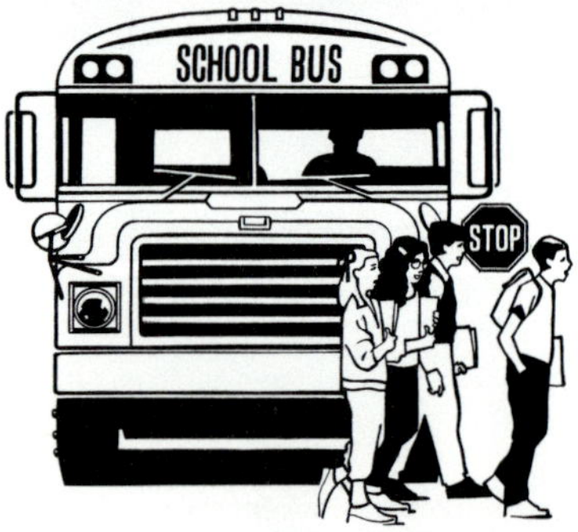

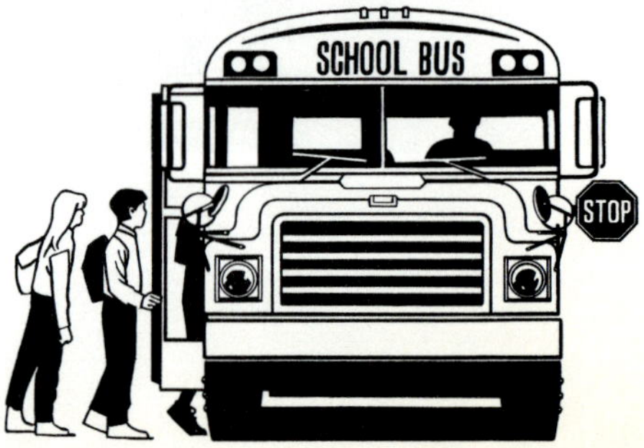

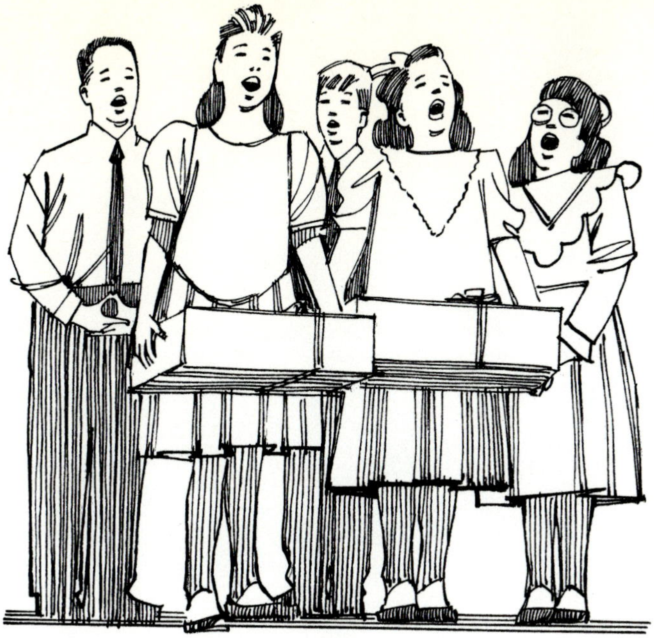

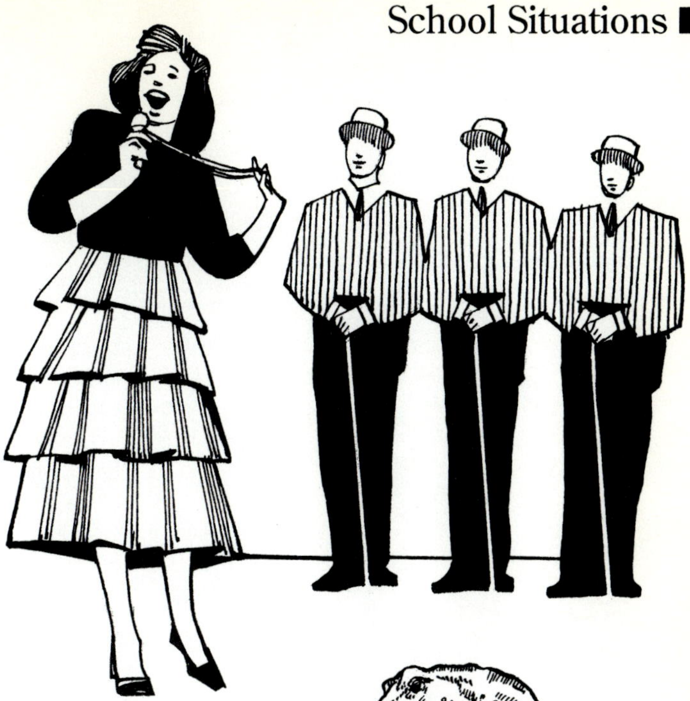

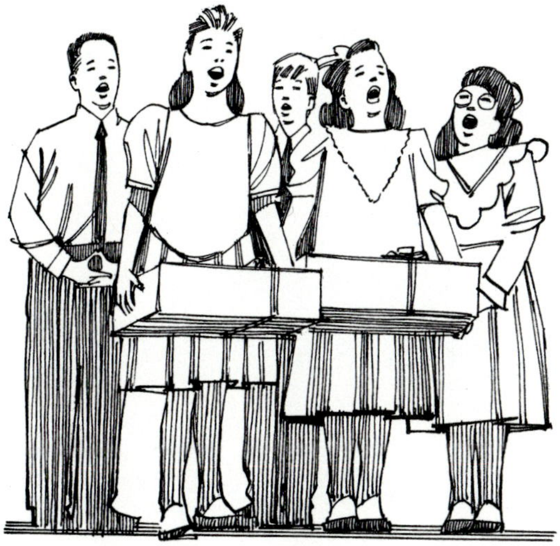

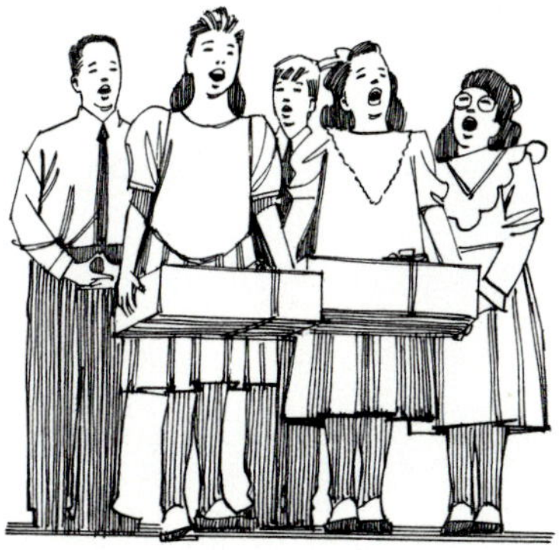

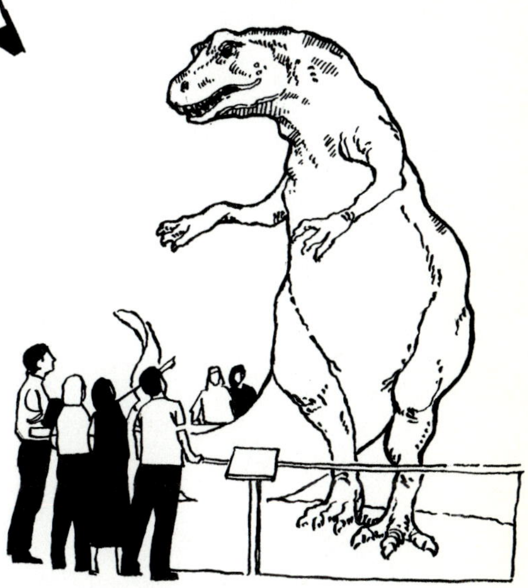

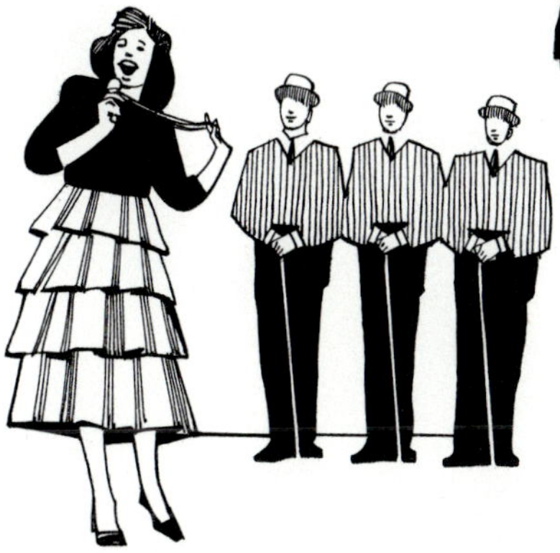

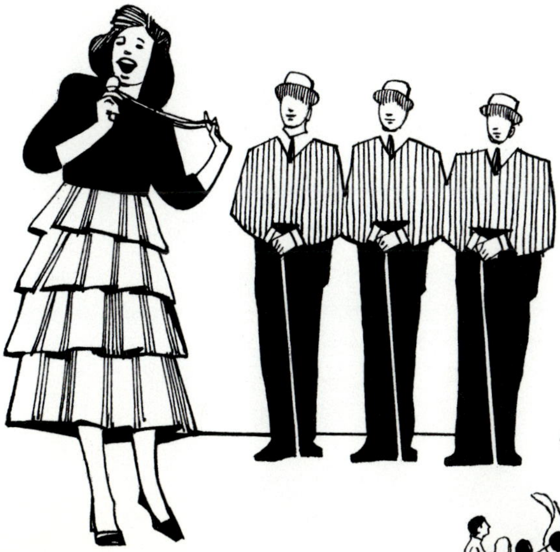

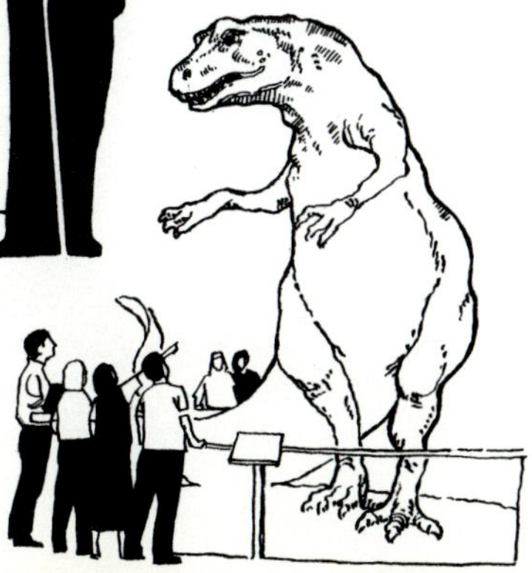

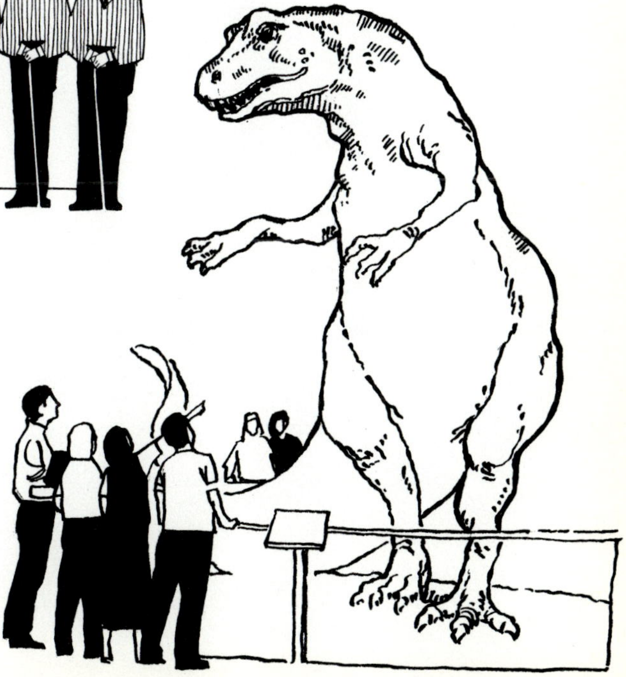

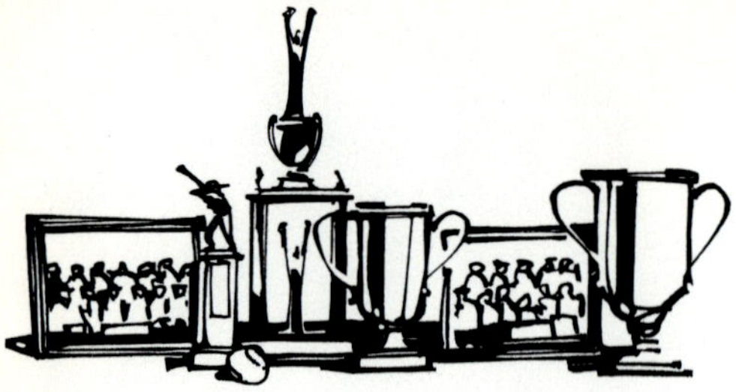

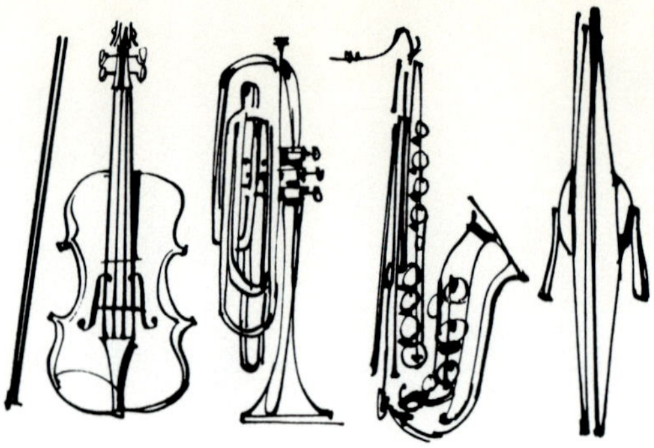

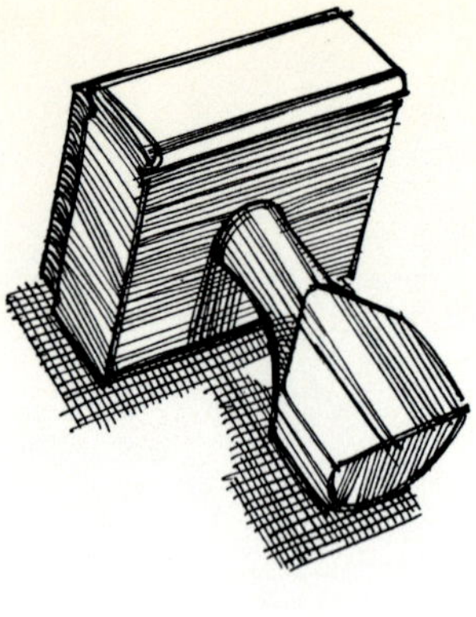

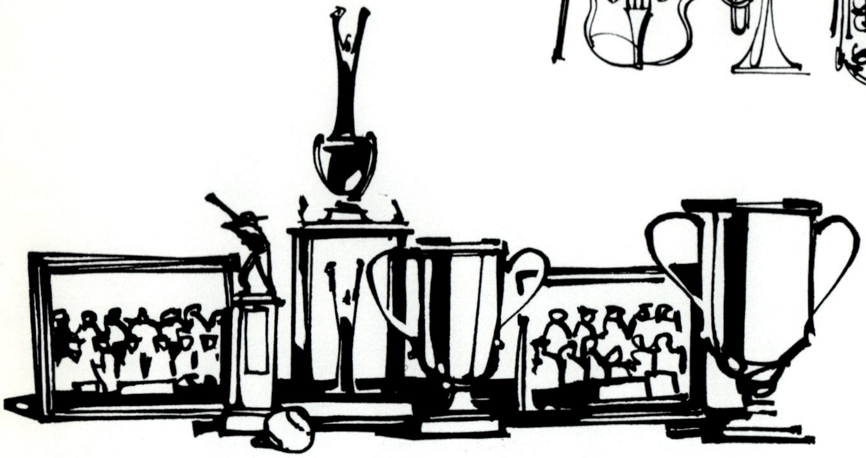

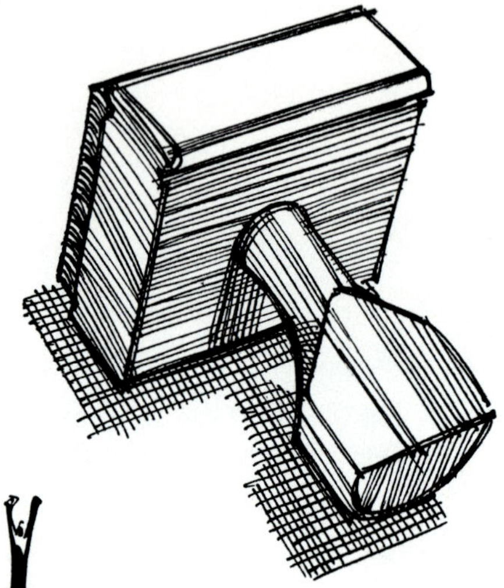

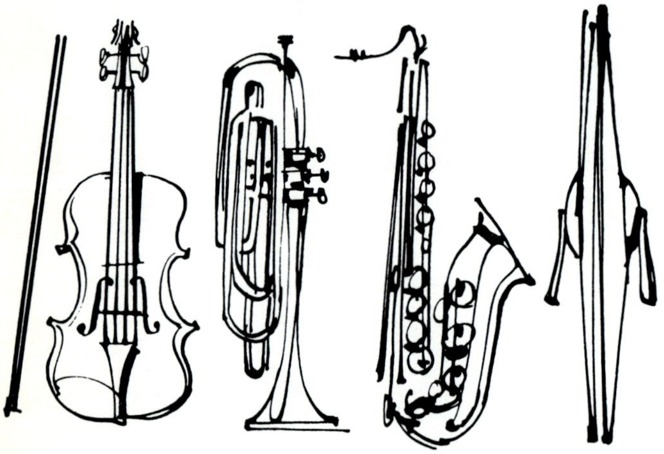

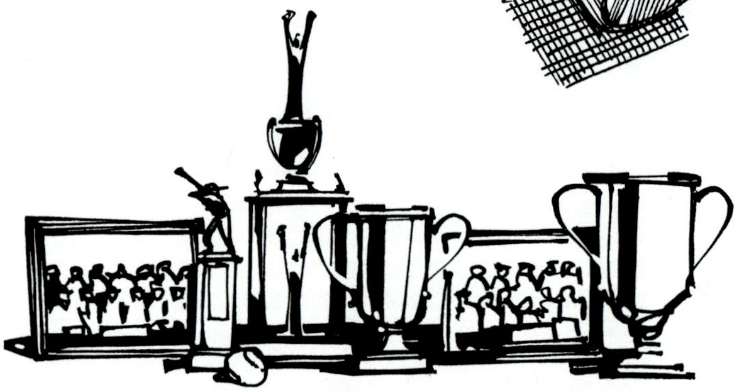

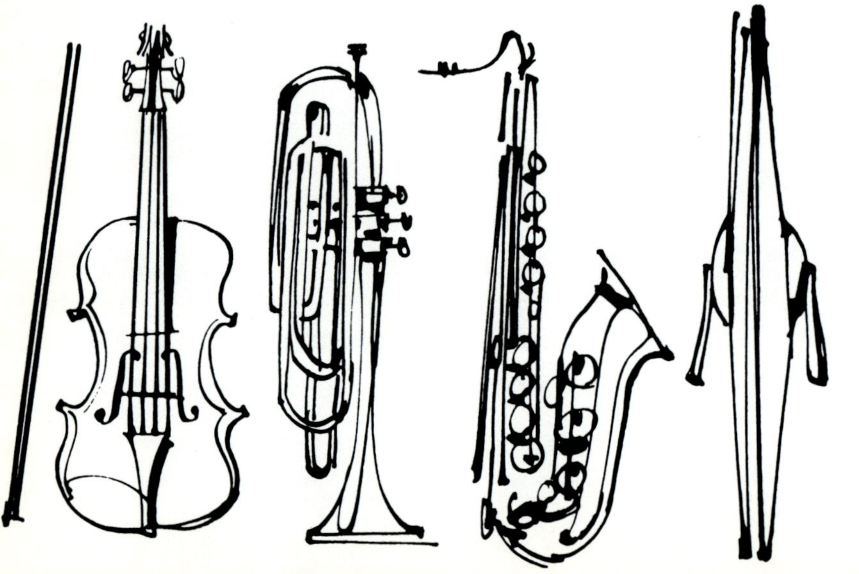

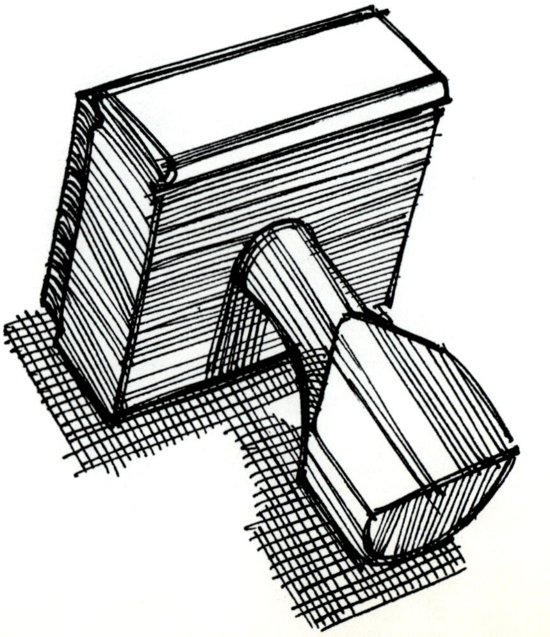

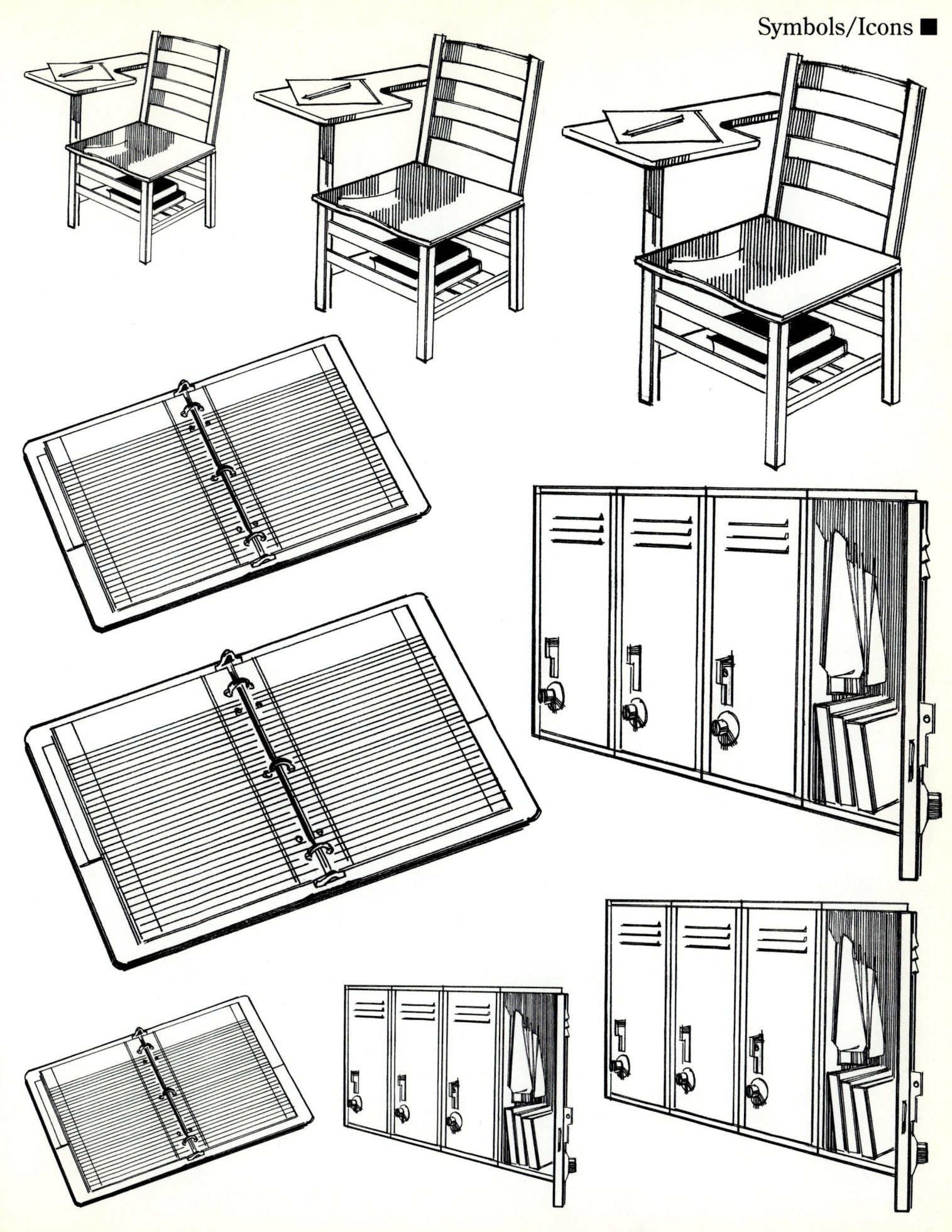

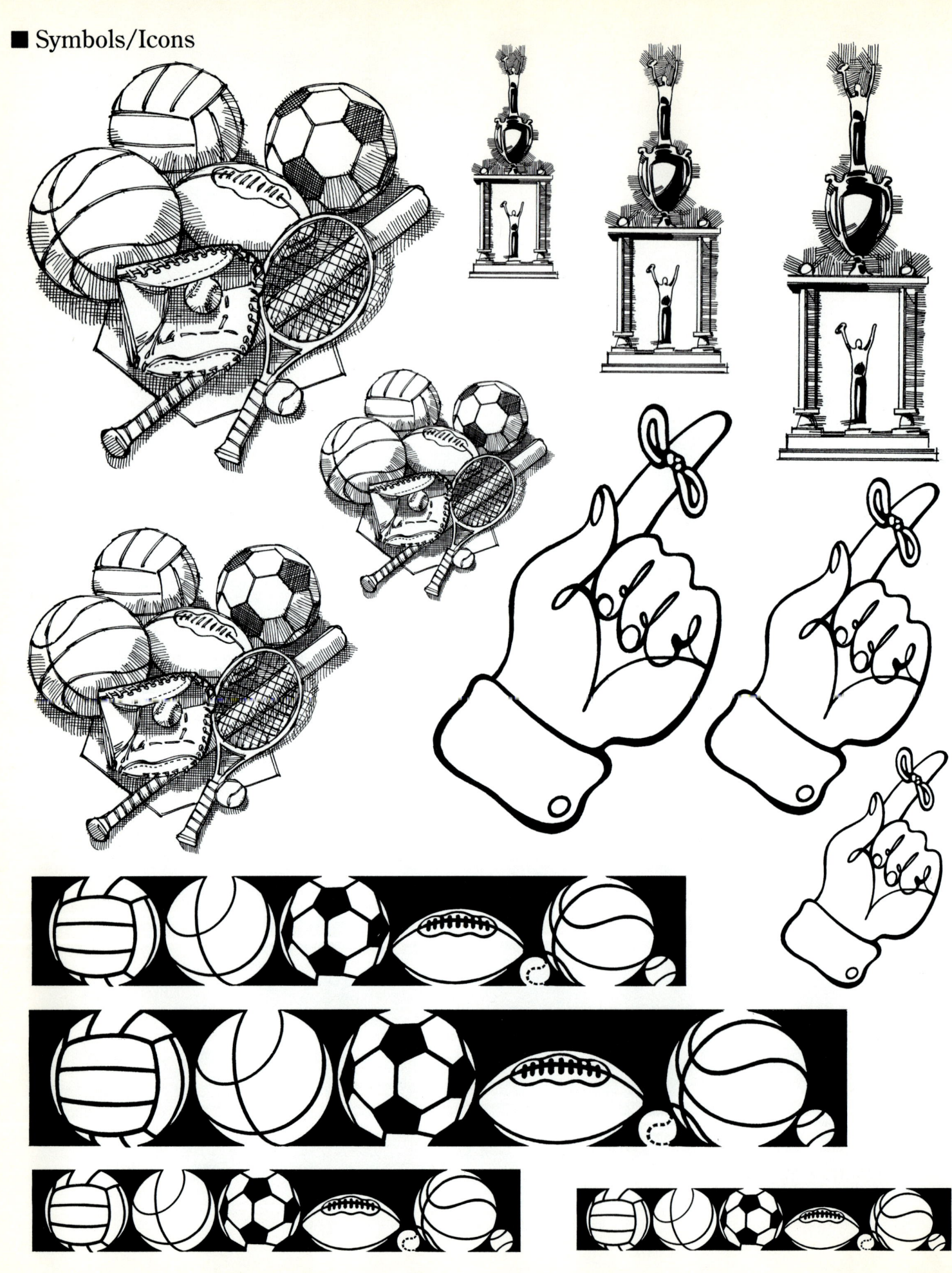

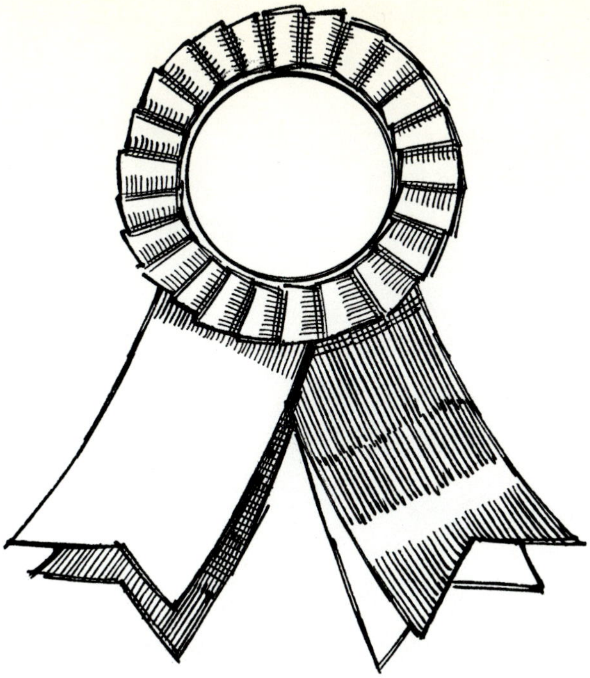

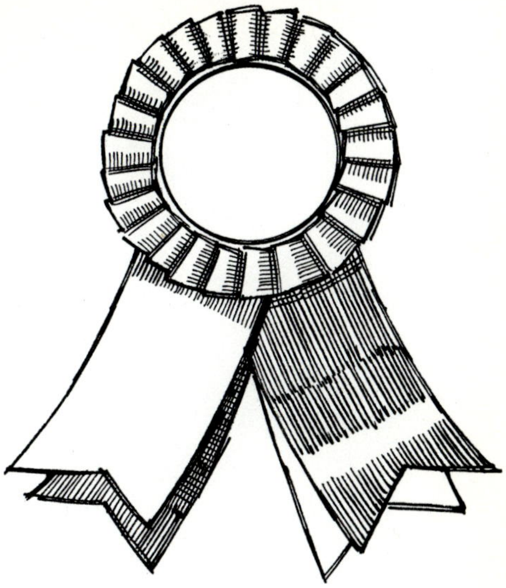

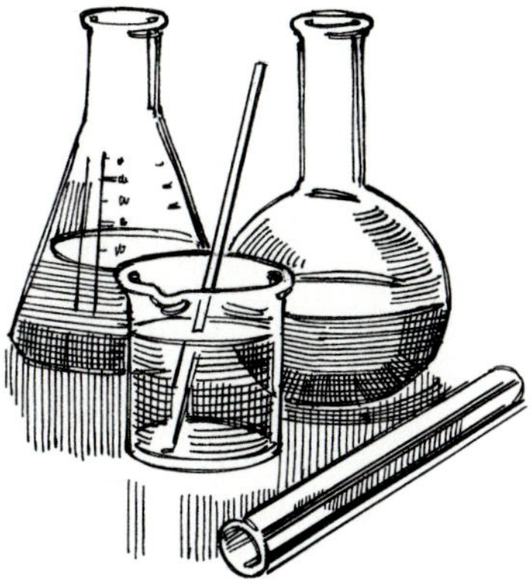

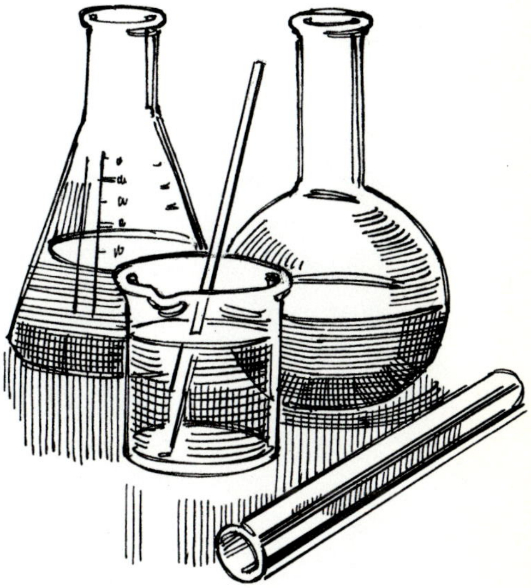

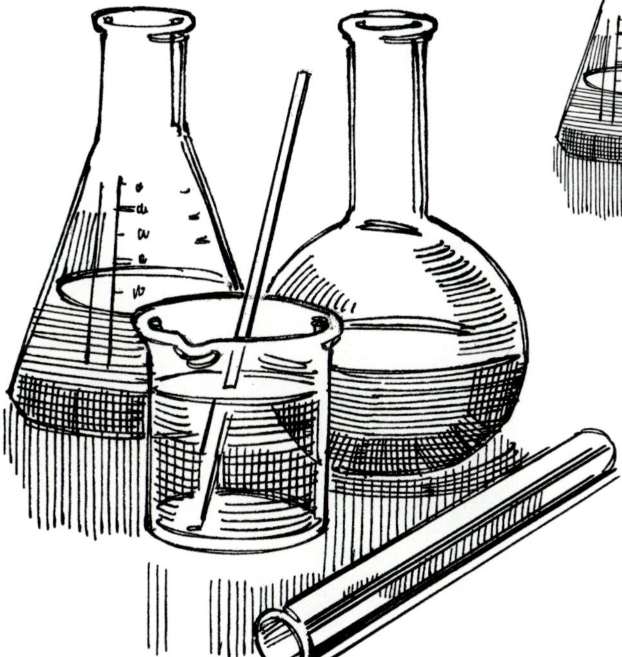

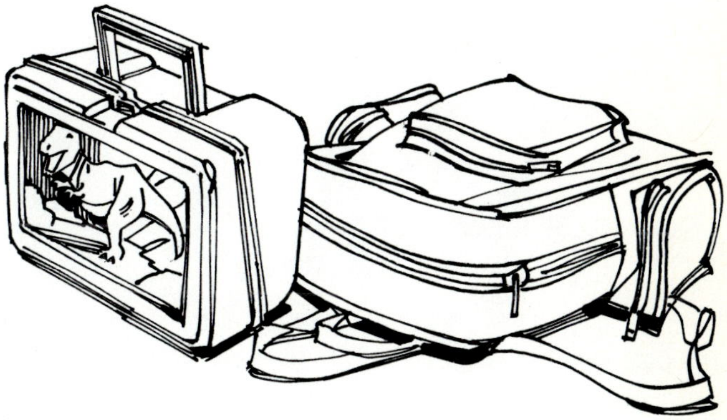

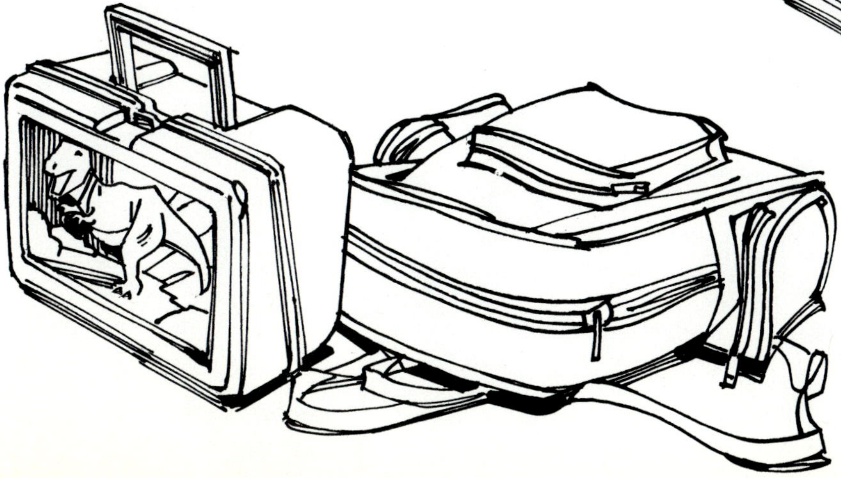

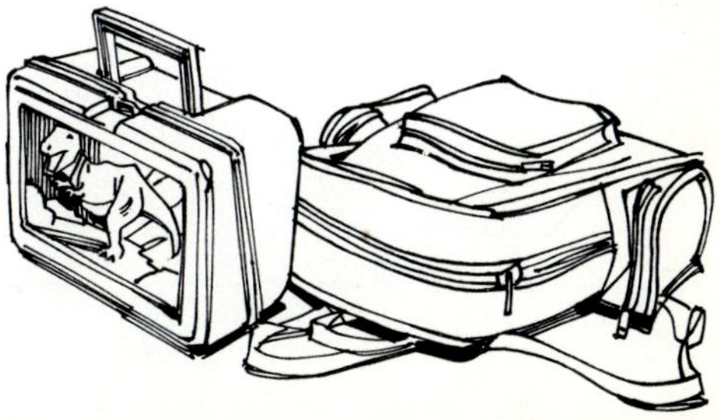

ASSIGNMENT BOOK

ASSIGNMENT BOOK

ASSIGNMENT BOOK

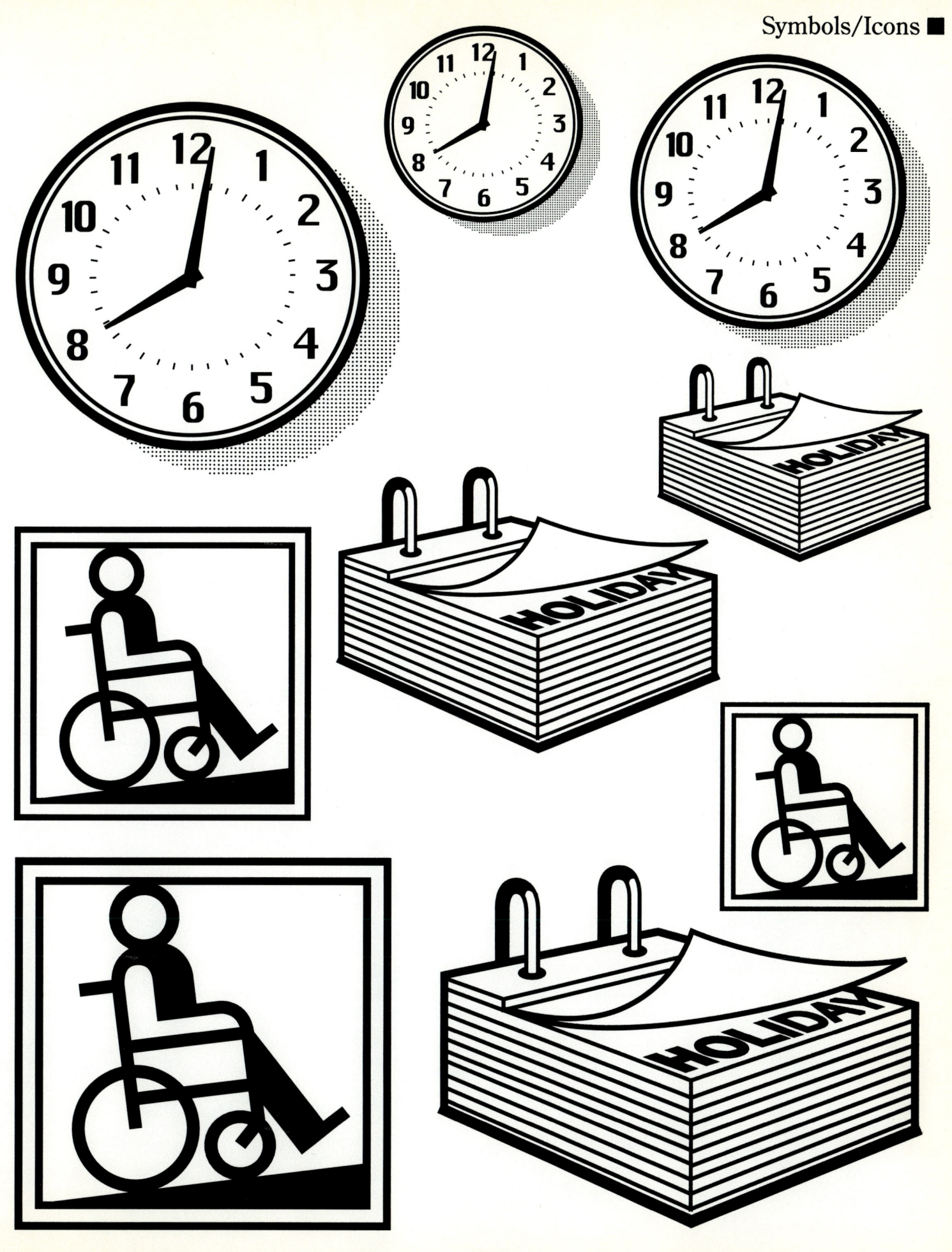

Symbols/Icons

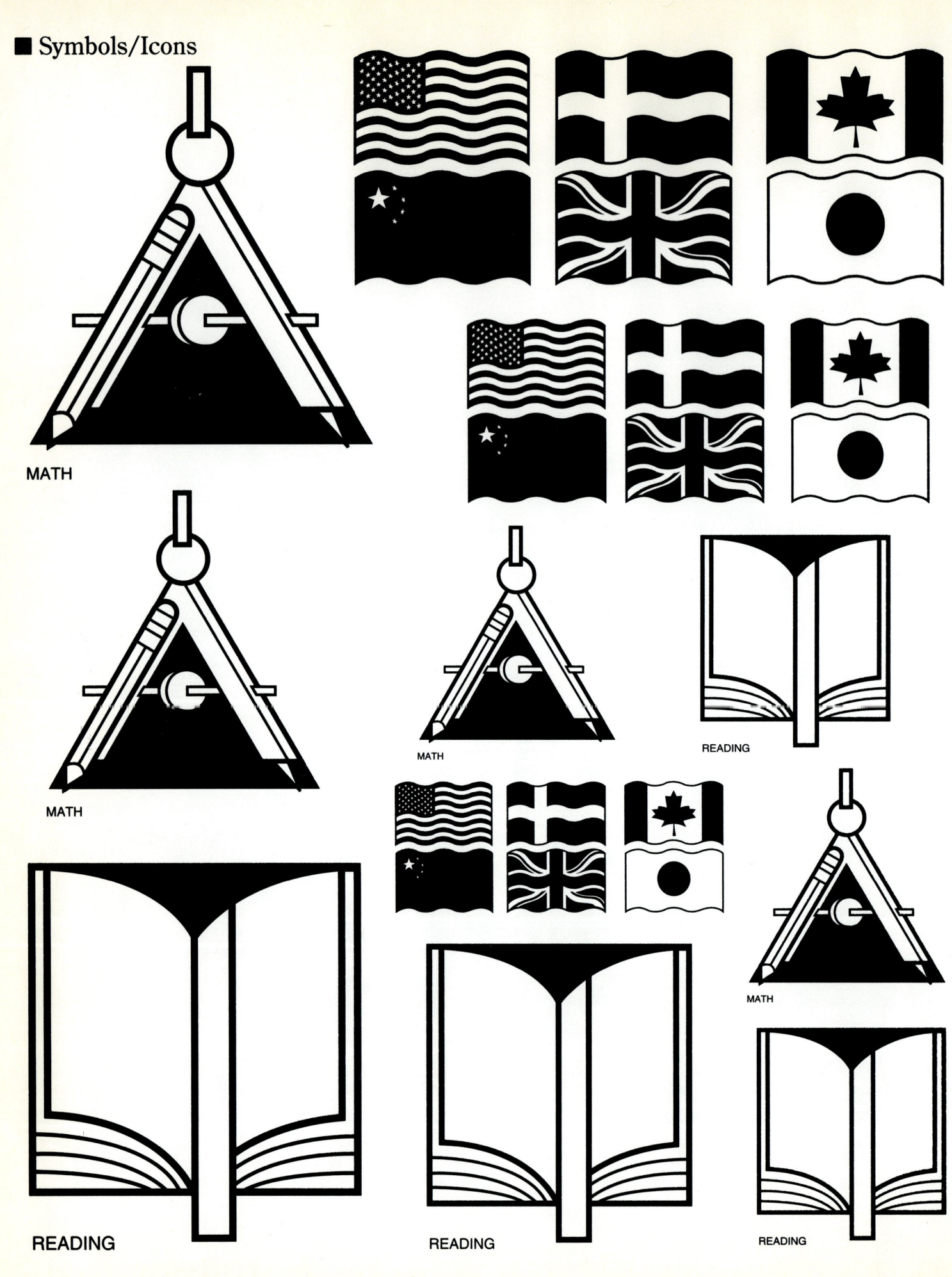

MATH

MATH

MATH

MATH

READING

READING

READING

READING

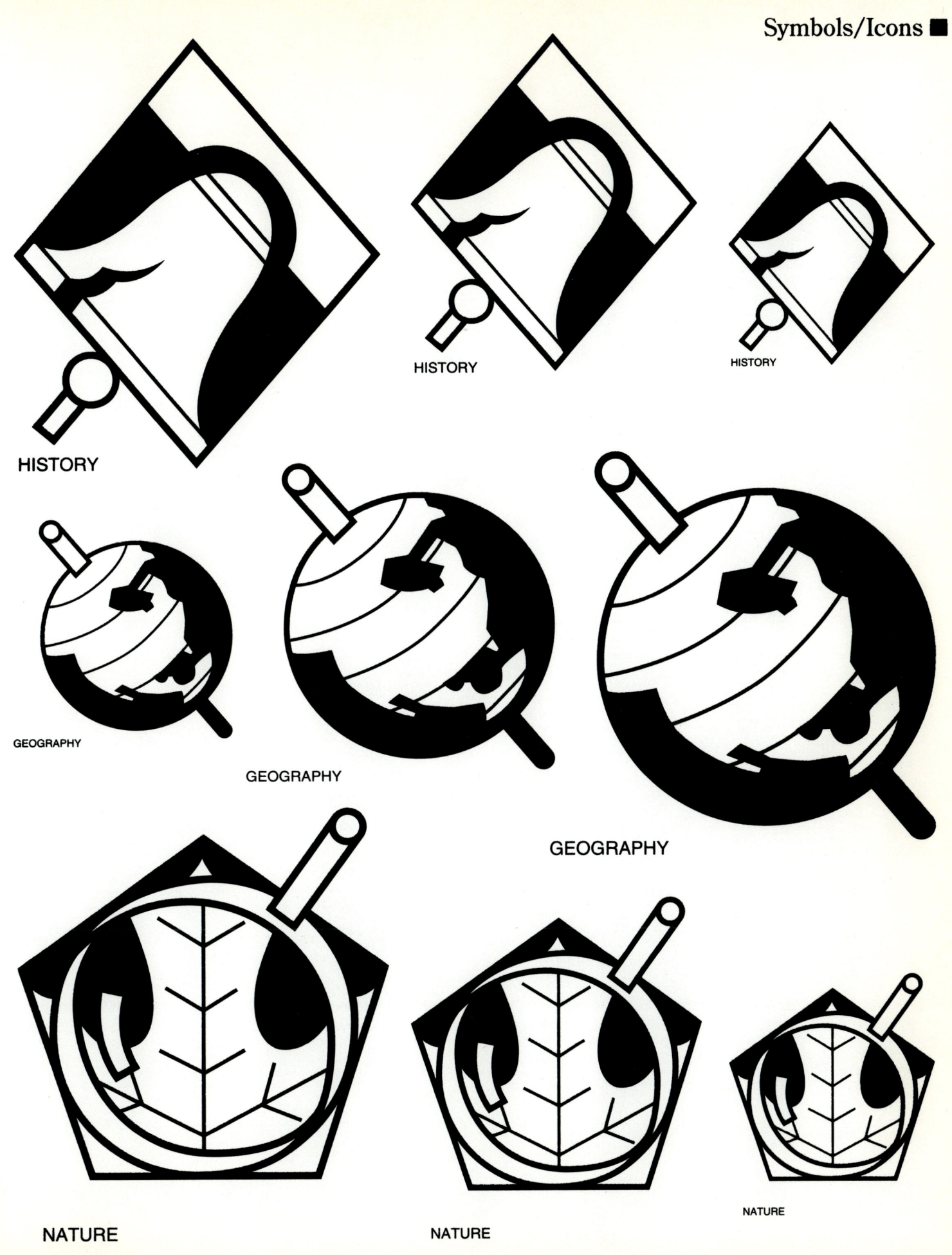

HISTORY

HISTORY

HISTORY

GEOGRAPHY

GEOGRAPHY

GEOGRAPHY

NATURE

NATURE

NATURE

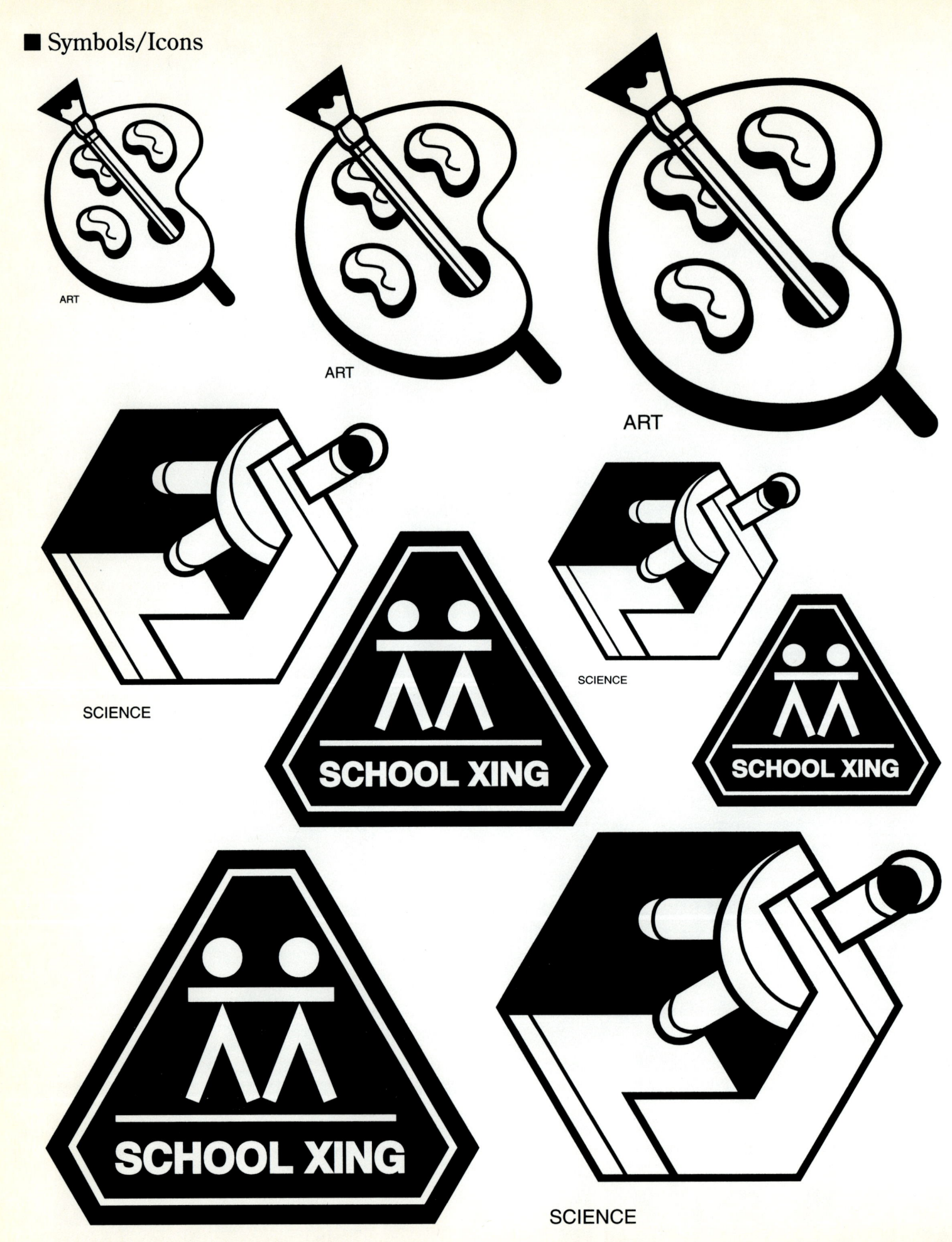

ART

ART

ART

SCIENCE

SCIENCE

SCHOOL XING

SCHOOL XING

SCHOOL XING

SCIENCE

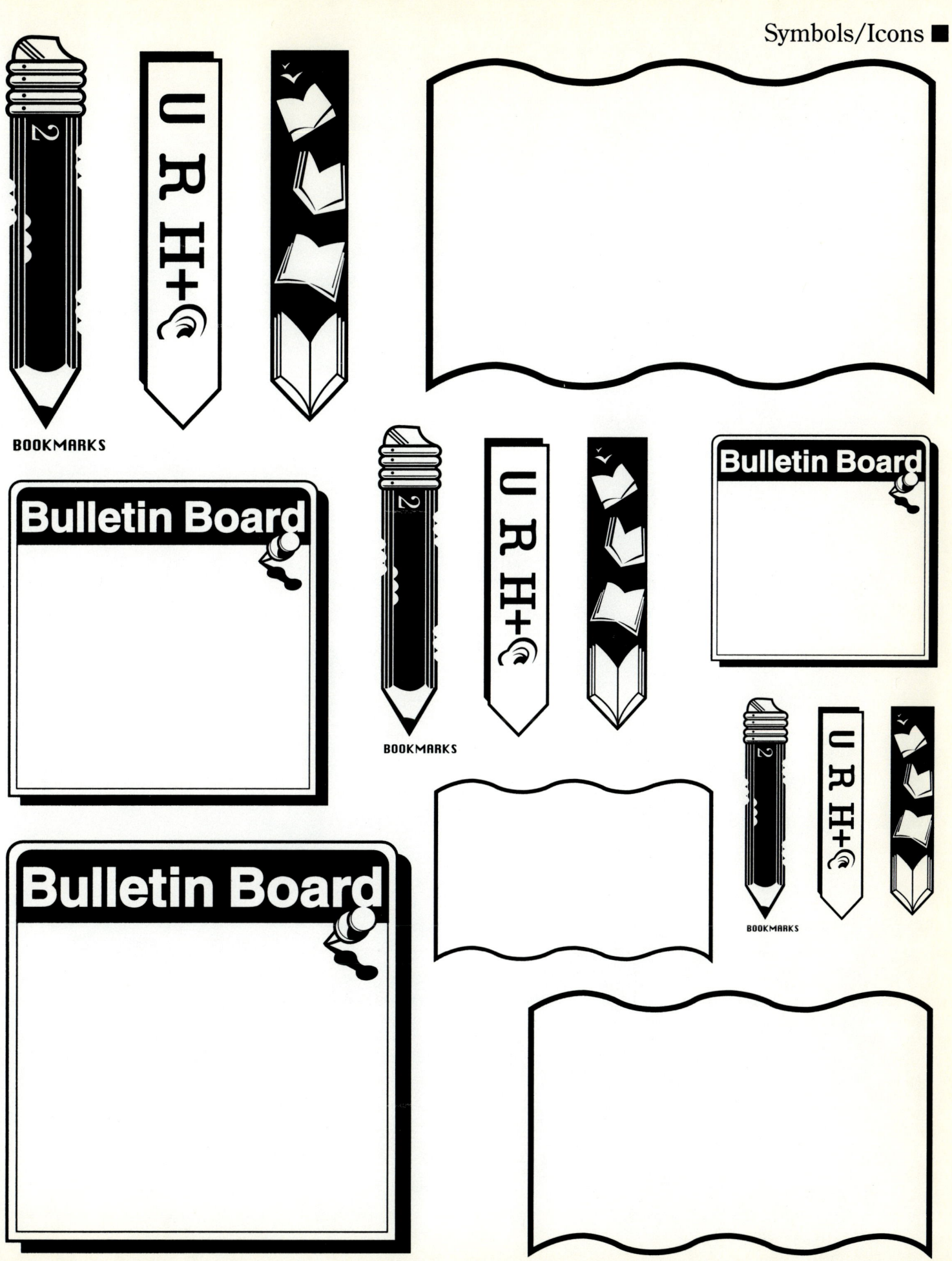

BOOKMARKS

Bulletin Board

BOOKMARKS

Bulletin Board

Bulletin Board

BOOKMARKS

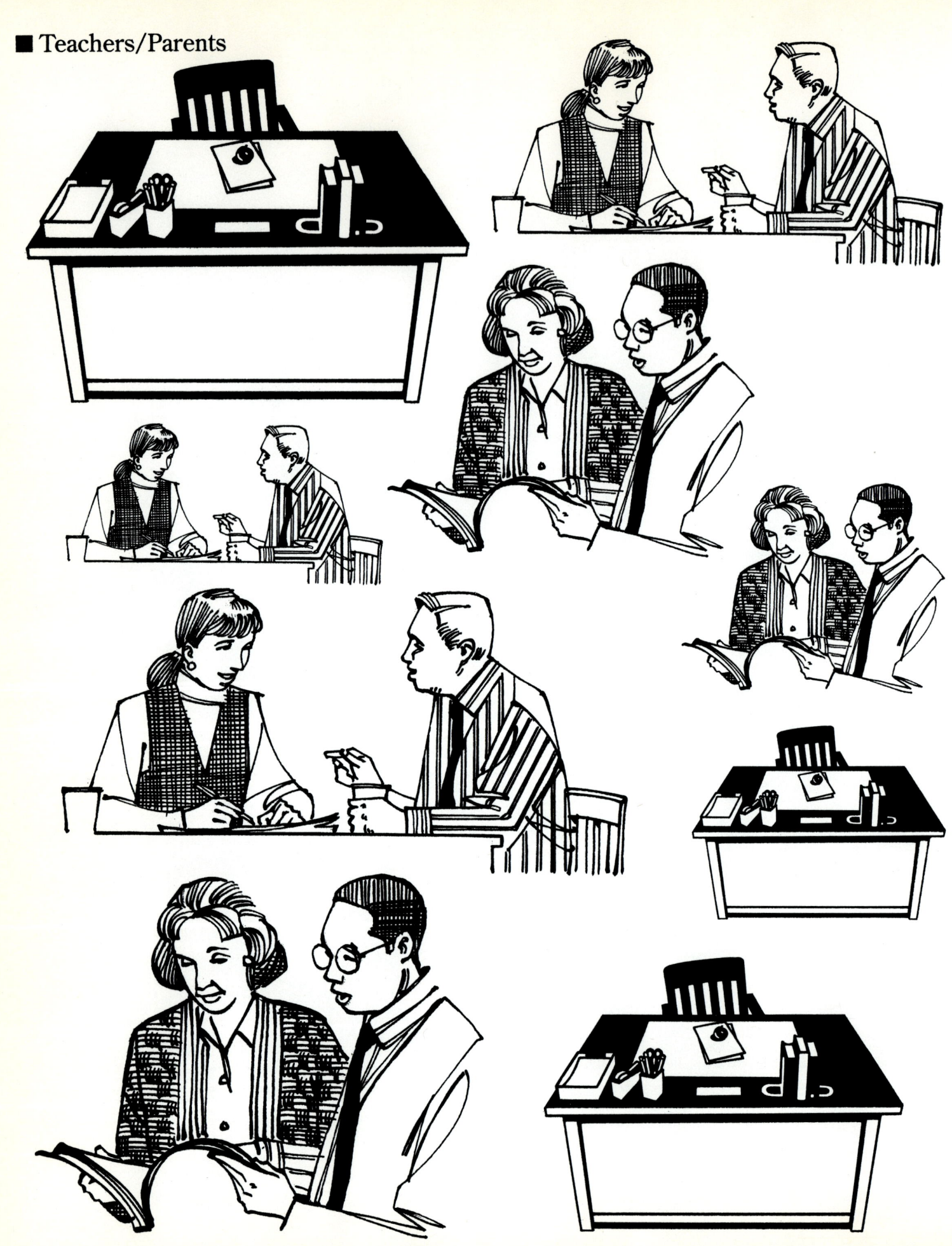

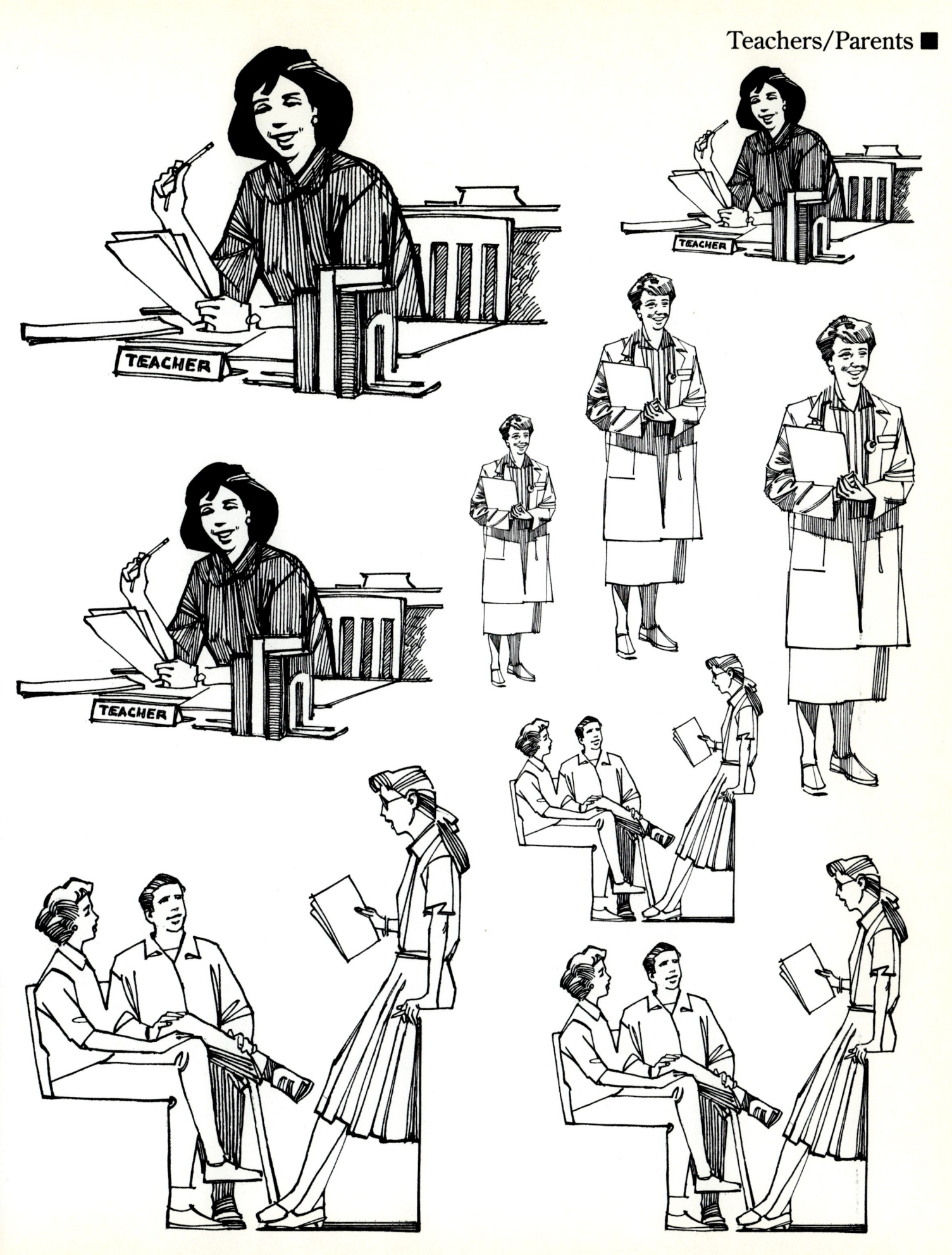

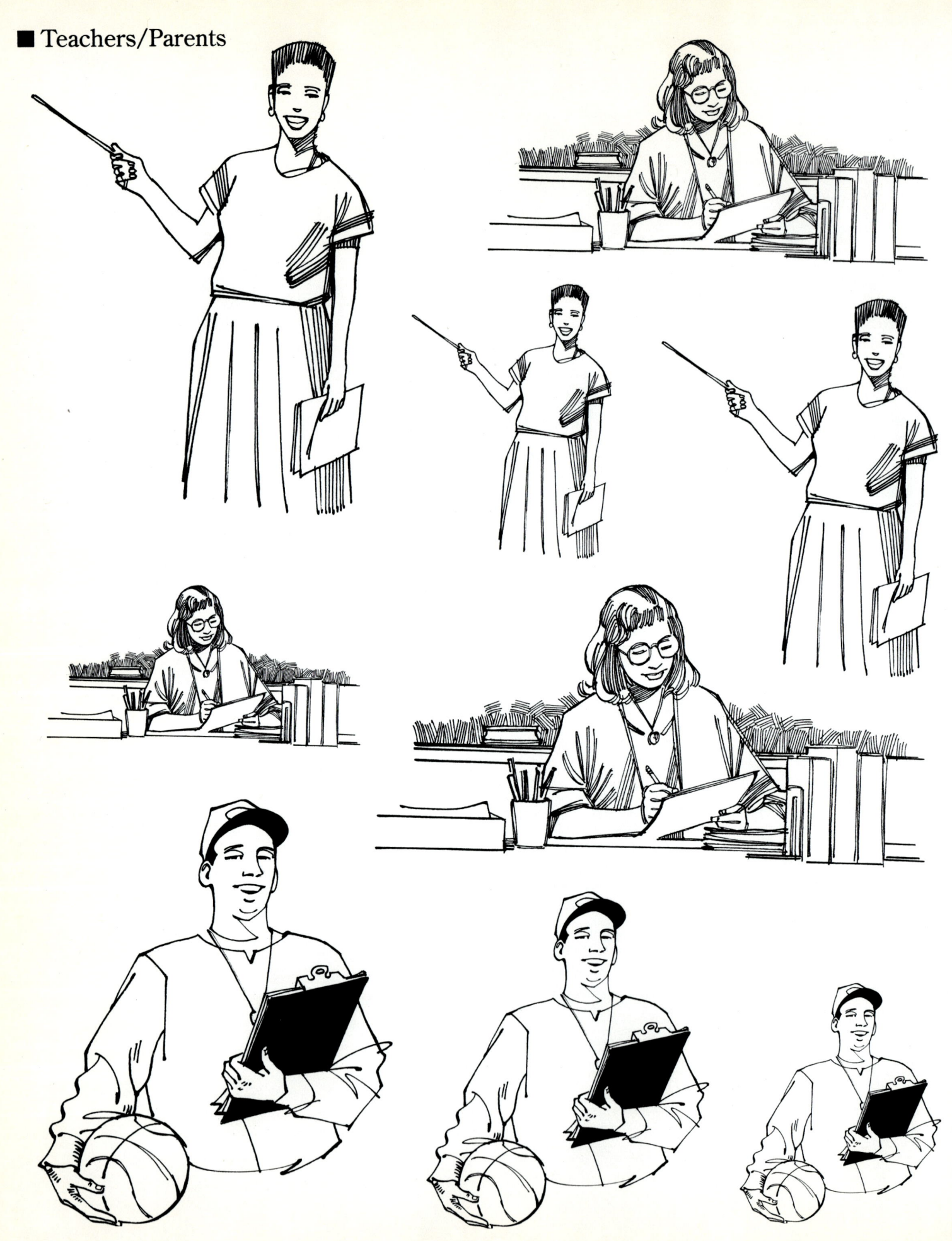